God's Wisdom®

for your

Every Need

Hi Michael,   2-10-2020

During your time being seperated from the love of your life, Shyanne. Now is your chance to get closer to your Father. Write in your journal share with Shyanne. Grow together with God's Word. This is worth more silver, gold or any riches. What is worth life? Love of God, Wife & Family.   We Love You Michael, take it one day at a time...

God's Wisdom®
for your
Every Need

COMPILED BY
Jack Countryman

Thomas Nelson
Since 1798

NASHVILLE DALLAS MEXICO CITY RIO DE JANEIRO

Published in Nashville, Tennessee, by Thomas Nelson.
Thomas Nelson® is a trademark of Thomas Nelson, Inc.

Thomas Nelson, Inc. titles may be purchased in
bulk for educational, business, fund-raising, or sales
promotional use. For information, please email
NelsonMinistryServices@ThomasNelson.com.

Cover and interior designed by Kristy Morell,
Smyrna, Tennessee.

ISBN-13: 9781404187559

ISBN-13: 9781404187573 (SE)

Printed in China

CONTENTS

PREFACE

Many years ago, we published *God's Promises for Your Every Need.* Our premise was that everyone *wants* to know what God has promised them and hopefully claim that promise. Today, we are faced with a culture that provides many challenges. We *need* to have God's wisdom, which will help us rise above whatever the world may present to Christians everywhere.

When God invited Solomon to ask for whatever he wanted, the king requested *wisdom* (1 Kings 3:9–12). That God-given wisdom taught Solomon that only a fool tries to solve life's problems without God's help.

God's guidance is more than sufficient for all the tests or trials we might face. We need only to seek it out in God's Word. In life, tests come in all shapes and sizes. Some we may anticipate; some may blindside us at the most unexpected times. Some tests require us to endure; others ask us to make the right decision immediately. Regardless of the package in which the test is wrapped, God instructs us to come to Him for the wisdom we so desperately need.

Life is full of choices and, if we want to make choices that glorify God and benefit us and others, we need God's guidance. Everyone eventually comes to a place in life where we desperately need God's wisdom.

When you seek God's wisdom through His Word, you will find the peace that passes all understanding and a confidence that you are making choices based on God's guidance. You may be the only one who will understand or agree with your decision, but you will have heard from the One who matters most. Choose God's wisdom.

Happy is the man who finds wisdom,
　　And the man who gains understanding;
For her proceeds are better than the profits
　　　　of silver,
　　And her gain than fine gold.
She is more precious than rubies,
　　And all the things you may desire cannot
　　　　compare with her.
Length of days is in her right hand,
　　In her left hand riches and honor.
Her ways are ways of pleasantness,
　　And all her paths are peace.
She is a tree of life to those who take hold
　　　　of her,
　　And happy are all who retain her.
　　　　　　　　　　　—Proverbs 3:13–18

Things to
Remember When . . .

Get wisdom! Get understanding!
   Do not forget, nor turn away from the
      words of my mouth.
Do not forsake her, and she will preserve
      you;
   Love her, and she will keep you.
Wisdom is the principal thing;
   Therefore get wisdom.
   And in all your getting, get
      understanding.

                    —PROVERBS 4:5–7

Things to Remember When
LIFE IS UNFAIR
IN THE WORKPLACE

And whatever you do, do it heartily, as to the Lord and not to men, knowing that from the Lord you will receive the reward of the inheritance; for you serve the Lord Christ. But he who does wrong will be repaid for what he has done, and there is no partiality.

—COLOSSIANS 3:23–25

And we urge you, brethren, to recognize those who labor among you, and are over you in the Lord and admonish you, and to esteem them very highly in love for their work's sake. Be at peace among yourselves. Now we exhort you, brethren, warn those who are unruly, comfort the fainthearted, uphold the weak, be patient with all. See that no one renders evil for evil to anyone, but always pursue what is good both for yourselves and for all.

—1 THESSALONIANS 5:12–15

Let nothing be done through selfish ambition or conceit, but in lowliness of mind let each esteem others better than himself. Let each of you look out not only for his own interests, but also for the interests of others.

—PHILIPPIANS 2:3–4

"Judge not, that you be not judged. For with what judgment you judge, you will be judged; and with the measure you use, it will be measured back to you.

"And why do you look at the speck in your brother's eye, but do not consider the plank in your own eye? Or how can you say to your brother, 'Let me remove the speck from your eye'; and look, a plank is in your own eye? Hypocrite! First remove the plank from your own eye, and then you will see clearly to remove the speck from your brother's eye."

—MATTHEW 7:1–5

Things to Remember When
YOUR WORLD IS
TURNED UPSIDE DOWN

Jesus answered them, "Do you now believe? Indeed the hour is coming, yes, has now come, that you will be scattered, each to his own, and will leave Me alone. And yet I am not alone, because the Father is with Me.

These things I have spoken to you, that in Me you may have peace. In the world you will have tribulation; but be of good cheer, I have overcome the world."

—JOHN 16:31–33

My brethren, count it all joy when you fall into various trials, knowing that the testing of your faith produces patience. But let patience have its perfect work, that you may be perfect and complete, lacking nothing. If any of you lacks wisdom, let him ask of God, who gives to all liberally and without reproach, and it will be given to him.

—JAMES 1:2–5

Therefore, having been justified by faith, we have peace with God through our Lord Jesus Christ, through whom also we have access by faith into this grace in which we stand, and rejoice in hope of the glory of God. And not only that, but we also glory in tribulations, knowing that tribulation produces perseverance; and perseverance, character; and character, hope. Now hope does not disappoint, because the love of God has been poured out in our hearts by the Holy Spirit who was given to us.

—ROMANS 5:1–5

Therefore we do not lose heart. Even though our outward man is perishing, yet the inward man is being renewed day by day. For our light affliction, which is but for a moment, is working for us a far more exceeding and eternal weight of glory, while we do not look at the things which are seen, but at the things which are not seen. For the things which are seen are temporary, but the things which are not seen are eternal.

—2 CORINTHIANS 4:16–18

Let love be without hypocrisy. Abhor what is evil. Cling to what is good. Be kindly affectionate to one another with brotherly love, in honor giving preference to one another; not lagging in diligence, fervent in spirit, serving the Lord; rejoicing in hope, patient in tribulation, continuing steadfastly in prayer.

—ROMANS 12:9–12

In everything give thanks; for this is the will of God in Christ Jesus for you.

Do not quench the Spirit. Do not despise prophecies. Test all things; hold fast what is good. Abstain from every form of evil.

—1 THESSALONIANS 5:18–22

Yet in all these things we are more than conquerors through Him who loved us. For I am persuaded that neither death nor life, nor angels nor principalities nor powers, nor things present nor things to come, nor height nor depth, nor any other created thing, shall be able to separate us from the love of God which is in Christ Jesus our Lord.

—ROMANS 8:37–39

Things to Remember When
Someone at Work
Gets under Your Skin

"For if you forgive men their trespasses,
your heavenly Father will also forgive you.
But if you do not forgive men their trespasses,
neither will your Father forgive your
trespasses."

—Matthew 6:14–15

"Take heed to yourselves. If your brother
sins against you, rebuke him; and if he repents,
forgive him. And if he sins against you seven
times in a day, and seven times in a day returns
to you, saying, 'I repent,' you shall forgive him."

—Luke 17:3–4

Then Peter came to Him and said, "Lord,
how often shall my brother sin against me, and
I forgive him? Up to seven times?"
Jesus said to him, "I do not say to you, up to
seven times, but up to seventy times seven."

—Matthew 18:21–22

"You have heard that it was said, '*You shall love your neighbor* and hate your enemy.' But I say to you, love your enemies, bless those who curse you, do good to those who hate you, and pray for those who spitefully use you and persecute you, that you may be sons of your Father in heaven; for He makes His sun rise on the evil and on the good, and sends rain on the just and on the unjust."

—MATTHEW 5:43–45

Finally, all of you be of one mind, having compassion for one another; love as brothers, be tenderhearted, be courteous; not returning evil for evil or reviling for reviling, but on the contrary blessing, knowing that you were called to this, that you may inherit a blessing.

—1 PETER 3:8–9

Cease from anger, and forsake wrath;
    Do not fret—it only causes harm.
For evildoers shall be cut off;
    But those who wait on the LORD,
    They shall inherit the earth.

—PSALM 37:8–9

Therefore, as the elect of God, holy and beloved, put on tender mercies, kindness, humility, meekness, longsuffering; bearing with one another, and forgiving one another, if anyone has a complaint against another; even as Christ forgave you, so you also must do. But above all these things put on love, which is the bond of perfection.

And let the peace of God rule in your hearts, to which also you were called in one body; and be thankful. Let the word of Christ dwell in you richly in all wisdom, teaching and admonishing one another in psalms and hymns and spiritual songs, singing with grace in your hearts to the Lord.

—COLOSSIANS 3:12–16

Things to Remember When
You Face
Disappointment in Life

In this you greatly rejoice, though now for a little while, if need be, you have been grieved by various trials, that the genuineness of your faith, being much more precious than gold that perishes, though it is tested by fire, may be found to praise, honor, and glory at the revelation of Jesus Christ, whom having not seen you love. Though now you do not see Him, yet believing, you rejoice with joy inexpressible and full of glory, receiving the end of your faith—the salvation of your souls.

—1 Peter 1:6–9

We are hard pressed on every side, yet not crushed; we are perplexed, but not in despair; persecuted, but not forsaken; struck down, but not destroyed—always carrying about in the body the dying of the Lord Jesus, that the life of Jesus also may be manifested in our body.

—2 Corinthians 4:8–10

Therefore do not cast away your confidence, which has great reward. For you have need of endurance, so that after you have done the will of God, you may receive the promise:

> *"For yet a little while,*
> *And He who is coming will come and will*
> *not tarry.*
> *Now the just shall live by faith;*
> *But if anyone draws back,*
> *My soul has no pleasure in him."*

—HEBREWS 10:35–38

Being confident of this very thing, that He who has begun a good work in you will complete it until the day of Jesus Christ.

—PHILIPPIANS 1:6

The LORD is near to those who have a
     broken heart,
    And saves such as have a contrite spirit.

Many are the afflictions of the righteous,
    But the LORD delivers him out of them all.

—PSALM 34:18–19

In the day when I cried out,
    You answered me,
And made me bold with
    strength in my soul.

Though I walk in the midst of trouble,
    You will revive me;
    You will stretch out Your hand
    Against the wrath of my enemies,
    And Your right hand will save me.
    The LORD will perfect that which concerns me;
    Your mercy, O LORD, endures forever;
    Do not forsake the works of Your hands.

—PSALM 138:3, 7–8

The steps of a good man are ordered by
        the LORD,
    And He delights in his way.
Though he fall, he shall not be utterly cast down;
    For the LORD upholds him with His hand.

I have been young, and *now* am old;
    Yet I have not seen the righteous forsaken,
    Nor his descendants begging bread.
He is ever merciful, and lends;
    And his descendants are blessed.

—PSALM 37:23–26

Things to Remember When
You Need to Share
the Lord with a Friend

For God has not given us a spirit of fear, but of power and of love and of a sound mind.

Therefore do not be ashamed of the testimony of our Lord, nor of me His prisoner, but share with me in the sufferings for the gospel according to the power of God, who has saved us and called us with a holy calling, not according to our works, but according to His own purpose and grace which was given to us in Christ Jesus before time began.

—2 Timothy 1:7–9

For I am not ashamed of the gospel of Christ, for it is the power of God to salvation for everyone who believes, for the Jew first and also for the Greek. For in it the righteousness of God is revealed from faith to faith; as it is written, *"The just shall live by faith."*

—Romans 1:16–17

"Do not fear therefore; you are of more value than many sparrows.

"Therefore whoever confesses Me before men, him I will also confess before My Father who is in heaven. But whoever denies Me before men, him I will also deny before My Father who is in heaven. . . . He who finds his life will lose it, and he who loses his life for My sake will find it."

—MATTHEW 10:31–33, 39

The fruit of the righteous is a tree of life,
   And he who wins souls is wise.

—PROVERBS 11:30

Brethren, if anyone among you wanders from the truth, and someone turns him back, let him know that he who turns a sinner from the error of his way will save a soul from death and cover a multitude of sins.

—JAMES 5:19–20

And this is the testimony: that God has given us eternal life, and this life is in His Son. He who has the Son has life; he who does not have the Son of God does not have life.

These things I have written to you who believe in the name of the Son of God, that you may know that you have eternal life, and that you may continue to believe in the name of the Son of God.

—1 JOHN 5:11–13

"For God so loved the world that He gave His only begotten Son, that whoever believes in Him should not perish but have everlasting life. For God did not send His Son into the world to condemn the world, but that the world through Him might be saved."

—JOHN 3:16–17

"Behold, I stand at the door and knock. If anyone hears My voice and opens the door, I will come in to him and dine with him, and he with Me. To him who overcomes I will grant to sit with Me on My throne, as I also overcame and sat down with My Father on His throne. He who has an ear, let him hear what the Spirit says to the churches."

—REVELATION 3:20–22

But God demonstrates His own love toward us, in that while we were still sinners, Christ died for us.

Much more then, having now been justified by His blood, we shall be saved from wrath through Him. For if when we were enemies we were reconciled to God through the death of His Son, much more, having been reconciled, we shall be saved by His life.

—ROMANS 5:8–10

Things to Remember When
YOU NEED
PATIENCE . . . NOW!

Servants, be submissive to your masters with all fear, not only to the good and gentle, but also to the harsh. For this is commendable, if because of conscience toward God one endures grief, suffering wrongfully. For what credit is it if, when you are beaten for your faults, you take it patiently? But when you do good and suffer, if you take it patiently, this is commendable before God. For to this you were called, because Christ also suffered for us, leaving us an example, that you should follow His steps.

—1 PETER 2:18–21

But, beloved, we are confident of better things concerning you, yes, things that accompany salvation, though we speak in this manner. . . . And we desire that each one of you show the same diligence to the full assurance of hope until the end, that you do not become sluggish, but imitate those who through faith and patience inherit the promises.

—HEBREWS 6:9, 11–12

Rest in the LORD, and wait patiently for Him;
　　Do not fret because of him who prospers
　　　　in his way,
　　Because of the man who brings wicked
　　　　schemes to pass.
Cease from anger, and forsake wrath;
　　Do not fret—it only causes harm.

The LORD knows the days of the upright,
　　And their inheritance shall be forever.

—PSALM 37:7–8, 18

He gives power to the weak,
　　And to those who have no might He
　　　　increases strength.
Even the youths shall faint and be weary,
　　And the young men shall utterly fall,
But those who wait on the LORD
　　Shall renew their strength;
　　They shall mount up with wings like eagles,
　　They shall run and not be weary,
　　They shall walk and not faint.

—ISAIAH 40:29–31

Consider the work of God;
    For who can make straight what He has
        made crooked?
In the day of prosperity be joyful,
    But in the day of adversity consider:
    Surely God has appointed the one as well as
        the other,
    So that man can find out nothing that will
        come after him.

—ECCLESIASTES 7:13–14

Therefore we also, since we are surrounded by so great a cloud of witnesses, let us lay aside every weight, and the sin which so easily ensnares us, and let us run with endurance the race that is set before us, looking unto Jesus, the author and finisher of our faith, who for the joy that was set before Him endured the cross, despising the shame, and has sat down at the right hand of the throne of God.

For consider Him who endured such hostility from sinners against Himself, lest you become weary and discouraged in your souls.

—HEBREWS 12:1–3

The LORD is near to all who call upon Him,
    To all who call upon Him in truth.
He will fulfill the desire of those who fear Him;
    He also will hear their cry and save them.

                              —PSALM 145:18–19

Things to Remember When
YOU ARE IN DOUBT
ABOUT WHAT TO SAY

He who has knowledge spares his words,
And a man of understanding is
of a calm spirit.
Even a fool is counted wise
when he holds his peace;
When he shuts his lips, he is
considered perceptive.
—PROVERBS 17:27–28

The words of a man's mouth are deep waters;
The wellspring of wisdom is a flowing
brook.

It is not good to show partiality to the wicked,
Or to overthrow the righteous in judgment.

A fool's lips enter into contention,
And his mouth calls for blows.
A fool's mouth is his destruction,
And his lips are the snare of his soul.
—PROVERBS 18:4–7

If a wise man contends with a foolish man,
    Whether the fool rages or laughs,
        there is no peace.
A fool vents all his feelings,
    But a wise man holds them back.

—PROVERBS 29:9, 11

"You are the light of the world. A city that is set on a hill cannot be hidden. Nor do they light a lamp and put it under a basket, but on a lampstand, and it gives light to all who are in the house. Let your light so shine before men, that they may see your good works and glorify your Father in heaven."

—MATTHEW 5:14–16

I said, "Age should speak,
    And multitude of years should teach wisdom."
But there is a spirit in man,
    And the breath of the Almighty gives
        him understanding.
Great men are not always wise,
    Nor do the aged always understand justice.

—JOB 32:7–9

To everything there is a season,
  A time for every purpose under heaven:

  A time to be born,
  And a time to die;
A time to plant,
  And a time to pluck what is planted;
A time to kill,
  And a time to heal;
A time to break down,
  And a time to build up;
A time to weep,
  And a time to laugh;
A time to mourn,
  And a time to dance;
A time to cast away stones,
  And a time to gather stones;
A time to embrace,
  And a time to refrain from embracing;
A time to gain,
  And a time to lose;
A time to keep,
  And a time to throw away;
A time to tear,
  And a time to sew;

A time to keep silence,
    And a time to speak;
A time to love,
    And a time to hate;
A time of war,
    And a time of peace.

                    —Ecclesiastes 3:1–8

Let my prayer be set before You as incense,
    The lifting up of my hands as the evening
        sacrifice.
Set a guard, O Lord, over my mouth;
    Keep watch over ther door of my lips.

                    Psalm 141:2–3

What to Do
When You Feel . . .

He who heeds the word wisely
    will find good,
    And whoever trusts in the LORD,
        happy is he.

The wise in heart will be called prudent,
    And sweetness of the lips
        increases learning.

The heart of the wise teaches his mouth,
    And adds learning to his lips.

Pleasant words are like a honeycomb,
    Sweetness to the soul and health to
        the bones.

—PROVERBS 16:20–21; 23–24

What to Do When You Feel
As If You Need
to Change Jobs

Likewise you younger people, submit yourselves to your elders. Yes, all of you be submissive to one another, and be clothed with humility, for

> *"God resists the proud,*
> *But gives grace to the humble."*

Therefore humble yourselves under the mighty hand of God, that He may exalt you in due time, casting all your care upon Him, for He cares for you.

Be sober, be vigilant; because your adversary the devil walks about like a roaring lion, seeking whom he may devour. Resist him, steadfast in the faith, knowing that the same sufferings are experienced by your brotherhood in the world.

But may the God of all grace, who called us to His eternal glory by Christ Jesus, after you have suffered a while, perfect, establish, strengthen, and settle you.

—1 Peter 5:5–10

What then shall we say to these things? If God is for us, who can be against us? He who did not spare His own Son, but delivered Him up for us all, how shall He not with Him also freely give us all things? Who shall bring a charge against God's elect? It is God who justifies. Who is he who condemns? It is Christ who died, and furthermore is also risen, who is even at the right hand of God, who also makes intercession for us. Who shall separate us from the love of Christ? Shall tribulation, or distress, or persecution, or famine, or nakedness, or peril, or sword? As it is written:

> *"For Your sake we are killed all day long;*
> *We are accounted as sheep for the slaughter."*

Yet in all these things we are more than conquerors through Him who loved us. For I am persuaded that neither death nor life, nor angels nor principalities nor powers, nor things present nor things to come, nor height nor depth, nor any other created thing, shall be able to separate us from the love of God which is in Christ Jesus our Lord.

—ROMANS 8:31–39

The LORD is my shepherd;
   I shall not want.
He makes me to lie down in green pastures;
   He leads me beside the still waters.
He restores my soul;
   He leads me in the paths of righteousness
For His name's sake.

Yea, though I walk through the valley of the
      shadow of death,

   I will fear no evil;
   For You are with me;
   Your rod and Your staff, they comfort me.

You prepare a table before me
   in the presence of my enemies;
   You anoint my head with oil;
   My cup runs over.
Surely goodness and mercy shall follow me
   All the days of my life;
   And I will dwell in the house of the LORD
      Forever.

—PSALM 23:1–6

The LORD is my light and my salvation;
   Whom shall I fear?

The LORD is the strength of my life;
Of whom shall I be afraid?
When the wicked came against me
To eat up my flesh,
My enemies and foes,
They stumbled and fell.
Though an army may encamp against me,
My heart shall not fear;
Though war may rise against me,
In this I will be confident.

Wait on the LORD;
Be of good courage,
And He shall strengthen your heart;
Wait, I say, on the LORD!

—PSALM 27:1–3, 14

But, beloved, we are confident of better things concerning you, yes, things that accompany salvation, though we speak in this manner. For God is not unjust to forget your work and labor of love which you have shown toward His name, in that you have ministered to the saints, and do minister. And we desire that each one of you show the same diligence to the full assurance of hope until the end, that you do not become sluggish, but imitate those who through faith and patience inherit the promises.

—HEBREWS 6:9–12

Therefore, my beloved, as you have always obeyed, not as in my presence only, but now much more in my absence, work out your own salvation with fear and trembling; for it is God who works in you both to will and to do for His good pleasure.

Do all things without complaining and disputing, that you may become blameless and harmless, children of God without fault in the midst of a crooked and perverse generation, among whom you shine as lights in the world, holding fast the word of life, so that I may rejoice in the day of Christ that I have not run in vain or labored in vain.

—PHILIPPIANS 2:12–16

What to Do When You Feel
YOU HAVE BEEN
BETRAYED BY A FRIEND

Love suffers long and is kind; love does not envy; love does not parade itself, is not puffed up; does not behave rudely, does not seek its own, is not provoked, thinks no evil; . . . bears all things, believes all things, hopes all things, endures all things.

Love never fails. But whether there are prophecies, they will fail; whether there are tongues, they will cease; whether there is knowledge, it will vanish away. . . . But when that which is perfect has come, then that which is in part will be done away.

—1 CORINTHIANS 13:4–5, 7–8, 10

Therefore, putting away lying, *"Let each one of you speak truth with his neighbor,"* for we are members of one another. *"Be angry, and do not sin"*: do not let the sun go down on your wrath, nor give place to the devil.

—EPHESIANS 4:25–27

Now we exhort you, brethren, warn those who are unruly, comfort the fainthearted, uphold the weak, be patient with all. See that no one renders evil for evil to anyone, but always pursue what is good both for yourselves and for all.

Rejoice always, pray without ceasing, in everything give thanks; for this is the will of God in Christ Jesus for you.

Do not quench the Spirit. Do not despise prophecies. Test all things; hold fast what is good.

—1 THESSALONIANS 5:14–21

"Therefore be merciful, just as your Father also is merciful.

"Judge not, and you shall not be judged. Condemn not, and you shall not be condemned. Forgive, and you will be forgiven. Give, and it will be given to you: good measure, pressed down, shaken together, and running over will be put into your bosom. For with the same measure that you use, it will be measured back to you."

—LUKE 6:36–38

Finally, all of you be of one mind, having compassion for one another; love as brothers, be tenderhearted, be courteous; not returning evil for evil or reviling for reviling, but on the contrary blessing, knowing that you were called to this, that you may inherit a blessing. For

> *"He who would love life*
> *And see good days,*
> *Let him refrain his tongue from evil,*
> *And his lips from speaking deceit.*
> *Let him turn away from evil and do good;*
> *Let him seek peace and pursue it.*
> *For the eyes of the LORD are on the righteous,*
> *And His ears are open to their prayers;*
> *But the face of the LORD is against those*
> *who do evil."*

—1 PETER 3:8–12

Be of the same mind toward one another. Do not set your mind on high things, but associate with the humble. Do not be wise in your own opinion.

Repay no one evil for evil. Have regard for good things in the sight of all men. If it is possible, as much as depends on you, live peaceably with all men. Beloved, do not avenge yourselves, but rather give place to wrath; for it is written, *"Vengeance is Mine, I will repay,"* says the Lord.

—ROMANS 12:16–19

"Therefore I say to you, whatever things you ask when you pray, believe that you receive them, and you will have them. And whenever you stand praying, if you have anything against anyone, forgive him, that your Father in heaven may also forgive you your trespasses. But if you do not forgive, neither will your Father in heaven forgive your trespasses."

—MARK 11:24–26

What to Do When You Feel
YOU WANT TO GIVE UP

Seeing then that we have a great High Priest who has passed through the heavens, Jesus the Son of God, let us hold fast our confession. For we do not have a High Priest who cannot sympathize with our weaknesses, but was in all points tempted as we are, yet without sin. Let us therefore come boldly to the throne of grace, that we may obtain mercy and find grace to help in time of need.

—HEBREWS 4:14–16

Not that I speak in regard to need, for I have learned in whatever state I am, to be content: I know how to be abased, and I know how to abound. Everywhere and in all things I have learned both to be full and to be hungry, both to abound and to suffer need. I can do all things through Christ who strengthens me.

—PHILIPPIANS 4:11–13

Fear not, for I am with you;
Be not dismayed, for I am your God.
I will strengthen you,
Yes, I will help you,
I will uphold you with My righteous right
hand.

—Isaiah 41:10

But thanks be to God, who gives us the
victory through our Lord Jesus Christ.
Therefore, my beloved brethren, be
steadfast, immovable, always abounding in the
work of the Lord, knowing that your labor is
not in vain in the Lord.

—1 Corinthians 15:57–58

Now thanks be to God who always leads us
in triumph in Christ, and through us diffuses
the fragrance of His knowledge in every place.
For we are to God the fragrance of Christ
among those who are being saved and among
those who are perishing. To the one we are the
aroma of death leading to death, and to the
other the aroma of life leading to life. And who
is sufficient for these things?

—2 Corinthians 2:14–16

My soul clings to the dust;
    Revive me according to Your word.
I have declared my ways, and You answered me;
    Teach me Your statutes.
Make me understand the way of Your precepts;
    So shall I meditate on Your wonderful works.
My soul melts from heaviness;
    Strengthen me according to Your word.
Remove from me the way of lying,
    And grant me Your law graciously.
I have chosen the way of truth;
    Your judgments I have laid before me.
I cling to Your testimonies;
    O LORD, do not put me to shame!
I will run the course of Your commandments,
    For You shall enlarge my heart.

—PSALM 119:25–32

    Brethren, I do not count myself to have apprehended; but one thing I do, forgetting those things which are behind and reaching forward to those things which are ahead, I press toward the goal for the prize of the upward call of God in Christ Jesus.

—PHILIPPIANS 3:13–14

He who dwells in the secret place
>   of the Most High
> Shall abide under the shadow of the Almighty.
I will say of the LORD, "He is my refuge and
>   my fortress;
> My God, in Him I will trust."
Surely He shall deliver you from the
>   snare of the fowler
> And from the perilous pestilence.
He shall cover you with His feathers,
>   And under His wings you shall take refuge;
>   His truth shall be your shield and buckler.
You shall not be afraid of the terror by night,
>   Nor of the arrow that flies by day,
Nor of the pestilence that walks in darkness,
>   Nor of the destruction that lays waste at
>   noonday.

A thousand may fall at your side,
>   And ten thousand at your right hand;
>   But it shall not come near you.

No evil shall befall you,
>   Nor shall any plague come near your dwelling;
For He shall give His angels charge over you,
>   To keep you in all your ways.

—PSALM 91:1–7, 10–11

"Behold, I have created the blacksmith
 Who blows the coals in the fire,
 Who brings forth an instrument for his work;
 And I have created the spoiler to destroy.
No weapon formed against you shall prosper,
 And every tongue which rises against
  you in judgment
 You shall condemn.
 This is the heritage of the servants of the LORD,
 And their righteousness *is* from Me,"
 Says the LORD.

—ISAIAH 54:16–17

What to Do When You Feel
Like Giving Someone
a Piece of Your Mind

Who is the man who desires life,
　　And loves many days, that he may see good?
Keep your tongue from evil,
　　And your lips from speaking deceit.
Depart from evil and do good;
　　Seek peace and pursue it.

　　　　　　　　　　　　　　—Psalm 34:12–14

All the ways of a man are pure in his own eyes,
　　But the Lord weighs the spirits.

Commit your works to the Lord,
　　And your thoughts will be established.

　　　　　　　　　　　　　　—Proverbs 16:2–3

He who follows righteousness and mercy
　　Finds life, righteousness and honor.

Whoever guards his mouth and tongue
　　Keeps his soul from troubles.

　　　　　　　　　　　　　　—Proverbs 21:21, 23

The wise in heart will be called prudent,
   And sweetness of the lips increases learning.

Understanding is a wellspring of life to him
      who has it.
   But the correction of fools is folly.

The heart of the wise teaches his mouth,
   And adds learning to his lips.
                              —PROVERBS 16:21–23

A man's stomach shall be satisfied from the
      fruit of his mouth;
   From the produce of his lips he shall be filled.

Death and life are in the power of the tongue,
   And those who love it will eat its fruit.
                              —PROVERBS 18:20–21

My son, give attention to my words;
   Incline your ear to my sayings.
Do not let them depart from your eyes;
   Keep them in the midst of your heart;
For they are life to those who find them,
   And health to all their flesh.
Keep your heart with all diligence,
   For out of it spring the issues of life.

Put away from you a deceitful mouth,
    And put perverse lips far from you.
Let your eyes look straight ahead,
    And your eyelids look right before you.
Ponder the path of your feet,
    And let all your ways be established.
Do not turn to the right or the left;
    Remove your foot from evil.

—PROVERBS 4:20–27

But no man can tame the tongue. It is an unruly evil, full of deadly poison.

With it we bless our God and Father, and with it we curse men, who have been made in the similitude of God. Out of the same mouth proceed blessing and cursing. My brethren, these things ought not to be so. Does a spring send forth fresh water and bitter from the same opening? Can a fig tree, my brethren, bear olives, or a grapevine bear figs? Thus no spring yields both salt water and fresh.

Who is wise and understanding among you? Let him show by good conduct that his works are done in the meekness of wisdom.

—JAMES 3:8–13

What to Do When You Feel
TOTALLY EXHAUSTED

Wait on the LORD,
    And keep His way,
    And He shall exalt you to inherit the land;
    When the wicked are cut off, you shall see it.
I have seen the wicked in great power,
    And spreading himself like a native
        green tree.
Yet he passed away, and behold, he was no more;
    Indeed I sought him, but he could not be
        found.

Mark the blameless man, and observe the
        upright;
    For the future of that man is peace.

But the salvation of the righteous is from
        the LORD;
    He is their strength in the time of trouble.
And the LORD shall help them and deliver them;
    He shall deliver them from the wicked,
    And save them,
    Because they trust in Him.

—PSALM 37:34–37, 39–40

In the day when I cried out, You answered me,
And made me bold with strength in my soul.

Though I walk in the midst of trouble,
You will revive me;
You will stretch out Your hand
Against the wrath of my enemies,
And Your right hand will save me.
The LORD will perfect that which concerns me;
Your mercy, O LORD, endures forever;
Do not forsake the works of Your hands.
—PSALM 138:3, 7–8

Bless the LORD, O my soul;
And all that is within me, bless His holy name!
Bless the LORD, O my soul,
And forget not all His benefits:
Who forgives all your iniquities,
Who heals all your diseases,
Who redeems your life from destruction,
Who crowns you with lovingkindness
and tender mercies,
Who satisfies your mouth with good things,
So that your youth is renewed like the eagle's.
—PSALM 103:1–5

Wait on the LORD;
    Be of good courage,
    And He shall strengthen your heart;
    Wait, I say, on the LORD!

—PSALM 27:14

For thus says the High and Lofty One
    Who inhabits eternity, whose name *is* Holy:
    "I dwell in the high and holy place,
    With him who has a contrite and humble
        spirit,
    To revive the spirit of the humble,
    And to revive the heart of the contrite ones."

"I have seen his ways, and will heal him;
    I will also lead him,
    And restore comforts to him
    And to his mourners.

"I create the fruit of the lips:
    Peace, peace to him who is far off and to
        him who is near,"
    Says the LORD,
    "And I will heal him."

—ISAIAH 57:15, 18–19

And let us not grow weary while doing good, for in due season we shall reap if we do not lose heart.

—GALATIANS 6:9

Take my yoke upon you and learn from Me, for I am gentle and lowly in heart, and you will find rest for your souls. For My yoke is easy and my burden is light.

—MATTHEW 11:29–30

What to Do When You Feel
LIKE NOT
COMING TO WORK

God is our refuge and strength,
 A very present help in trouble.
Therefore we will not fear,
 Even though the earth be removed,
 And though the mountains be carried into
  the midst of the sea;
Though its waters roar and be troubled,
 Though the mountains shake with its swelling.

There is a river whose streams shall make
  glad the city of God,
 The holy place of the tabernacle of the
  Most High.
God is in the midst of her, she shall not be moved;
 God shall help her, just at the break of dawn.

—PSALM 46:1–5

Therefore strengthen the hands which hang
down, and the feeble knees.

—HEBREWS 12:12

Be anxious for nothing, but in everything by prayer and supplication, with thanksgiving, let your requests be made known to God; and the peace of God, which surpasses all understanding, will guard your hearts and minds through Christ Jesus.

—PHILIPPIANS 4:6–7

Sing praise to the LORD, you saints of His,
    And give thanks at the remembrance of
        His holy name.
For His anger is but for a moment,
    His favor is for life;
    Weeping may endure for a night,
    But joy comes in the morning.

—PSALM 30:4–5

Our soul waits for the LORD;
    He is our help and our shield.
For our heart shall rejoice in Him,
    Because we have trusted in His holy name.
Let Your mercy, O LORD, be upon us,
    Just as we hope in You.

—PSALM 33:20–22

Praise the LORD!
  For it is good to sing praises to our God;
  For it is pleasant, and praise is beautiful.

He heals the brokenhearted
  And binds up their wounds.
He counts the number of the stars;
  He calls them all by name.
Great is our LORD, and mighty in power;
  His understanding is infinite.
The LORD lifts up the humble;
  He casts the wicked down to the ground.

—PSALM 147:1, 3–6

"Six days you shall work, but on the seventh day you shall rest; in plowing time and in harvest you shall rest."

—EXODUS 34:21

And God is able to make all grace abound toward you, always having all sufficiency in all things, may have an abundance for every good work.

—2 CORINTHIANS 9:8

For if anyone thinks himself to be something, when he is nothing, he deceives himself. But let each one examine his own work, and then he will have rejoicing in himself alone, and not in another. For each one shall bear his own load.

—GALATIANS 6:3–5

For we are God's fellow workers; you are God's field, you are God's building.

—1 CORINTHIANS 3:9

But we urge you, brethren, . . . that you also aspire to lead a quiet life, to mind your own business, and to work with your own hands, as we commanded you, that you may walk properly toward those who are outside, and that you may lack nothing.

—1 THESSALONIANS 4:10–12

What You Should Know When . . .

Teach me, O LORD, the way of
        Your statutes,
    And I shall keep it to the end.
Give me understanding, and I shall keep
        Your law;
    Indeed, I shall observe it with my
        whole heart.
Make me walk in the path of Your
        commandments,
    For I delight in it.

—PSALM 119:33–35

What You Should Know When
DIFFICULT DECISIONS
HAVE TO BE MADE

I will lift up my eyes to the hills—
From whence comes my help?
My help comes from the LORD,
Who made heaven and earth.

He will not allow your foot to be moved;
He who keeps you will not slumber.
Behold, He who keeps Israel
Shall neither slumber nor sleep.

The LORD is your keeper;
The LORD is your shade at your right hand.
The sun shall not strike you by day,
Nor the moon by night.

The LORD shall preserve you from all evil;
He shall preserve your soul.
The LORD shall preserve your going out
and your coming in
From this time forth, and even forevermore.

—PSALM 121

I will be glad and rejoice in Your mercy,
    For You have considered my trouble;
    You have known my soul in adversities,
And have not shut me up into the hand of
        the enemy;
    You have set my feet in a wide place.
                            —Psalm 31:7–8

The preparations of the heart belong to man,
    But the answer of the tongue is from the
        Lord.

All the ways of a man are pure in his own eyes,
    But the Lord weighs the spirits.

Commit your works to the Lord,
    And your thoughts will be established.

When a man's ways please the Lord,
    He makes even his enemies to be at peace
        with him.

Better is a little with righteousness,
    Than vast revenues without justice.

A man's heart plans his way,
    But the Lord directs his steps.
                        —Proverbs 16:1–3, 7–9

My son, keep your father's command,
    And do not forsake the law of your mother.
Bind them continually upon your heart;
    Tie them around your neck.
When you roam, they will lead you;
    When you sleep, they will keep you;
    And when you awake, they will speak
        with you.
For the commandment is a lamp,
    And the law a light;
    Reproofs of instruction are the way of life.

—PROVERBS 6:20–23

Deal bountifully with Your servant,
    That I may live and keep Your word.
Open my eyes, that I may see
    Wondrous things from Your law.
I am a stranger in the earth;
    Do not hide Your commandments from me.
My soul breaks with longing
    For Your judgments at all times.

Your testimonies also are my delight
    And my counselors.

—PSALM 119:17–20, 24

O God, You are my God;
    Early will I seek You;
    My soul thirsts for You;
    My flesh longs for You
    In a dry and thirsty land
    Where there is no water.
So I have looked for You in the sanctuary,
    To see Your power and Your glory.

Because Your lovingkindness is better than life,
    My lips shall praise You.
Thus I will bless You while I live;
    I will lift up my hands in Your name.
My soul shall be satisfied as with marrow
            and fatness,
        And my mouth shall praise You with
            joyful lips.

—Psalm 63:1–5

I will bless the Lord who has given me counsel;
    My heart also instructs me in the night
            seasons.
I have set the Lord always before me;
    Because He is at my right hand I shall not
        be moved.

Therefore my heart is glad, and my glory rejoices;
  My flesh also will rest in hope.
For You will not leave my soul in Sheol,
  Nor will You allow Your Holy One to see
    corruption.
You will show me the path of life;
  In Your presence is fullness of joy;
At Your right hand are pleasures forevermore.

—PSALM 16:7–11

What You Should Know When
YOU ARE SUDDENLY
OUT OF WORK

The young lions lack and suffer hunger;
>But those who seek the LORD shall not lack
>>any good thing.

—PSALM 34:10

He shall bring forth your righteousness as
>>the light,
>And your justice as the noonday.

Rest in the LORD, and wait patiently for Him;
>Do not fret because of him who prospers in
>>his way,
>Because of the man who brings wicked
>>schemes to pass.
Cease from anger, and forsake wrath;
>Do not fret—it only causes harm.

For evildoers shall be cut off;
>But those who wait on the LORD,
>They shall inherit the earth.

—PSALM 37:6–9

I waited patiently for the LORD;
    And He inclined to me,
    And heard my cry.
He also brought me up out of a horrible pit,
    Out of the miry clay,
    And set my feet upon a rock,
    And established my steps.
He has put a new song in my mouth—
    Praise to our God;
    Many will see it and fear,
    And will trust in the LORD.

Blessed is that man who makes the LORD his
       trust,
    And does not respect the proud, nor such as
       turn aside to lies.
Many, O LORD my God, are Your wonderful
       works
    Which You have done;
    And Your thoughts toward us
    Cannot be recounted to You in order;
    If I would declare and speak of them,
    They are more than can be numbered.

                    —PSALM 40:1–5

The LORD is good,
    A stronghold in the day of trouble;
    And He knows those who trust in Him.

                    —NAHUM 1:7

"Let not your heart be troubled; you believe in God, believe also in Me. In My Father's house are many mansions; if it were not so, I would have told you. I go to prepare a place for you. And if I go and prepare a place for you, I will come again and receive you to Myself; that where I am, there you may be also."

—JOHN 14:1–3

My son, give attention to my words;
    Incline your ear to my sayings.
Do not let them depart from your eyes;
    Keep them in the midst of your heart;
For they are life to those who find them,
    And health to all their flesh.
Keep your heart with all diligence,
    For out of it spring the issues of life.

—PROVERBS 4:20–23

O LORD, You have searched me and known me.
You know my sitting down and my rising up;
    You understand my thought afar off.
You comprehend my path and my lying down,
    And are acquainted with all my ways.
For there is not a word on my tongue,
    But behold, O LORD, You know it altogether.

You have hedged me behind and before,
    And laid Your hand upon me.
Such knowledge is too wonderful for me;
    It is high, I cannot attain it.

Where can I go from Your Spirit?
    Or where can I flee from Your presence?
If I ascend into heaven, You are there;
    If I make my bed in hell, behold, You are there.
If I take the wings of the morning,
    And dwell in the uttermost parts of the sea,
Even there Your hand shall lead me,
    And Your right hand shall hold me.
If I say, "Surely the darkness shall fall on me,"
    Even the night shall be light about me;
Indeed, the darkness shall not hide from You,
    But the night shines as the day;
    The darkness and the light are both alike
        to You.

Search me, O God, and know my heart;
    Try me, and know my anxieties;
And see if there is any wicked way in me,
    And lead me in the way everlasting.

—PSALM 139:1–12, 23–24

What You Should Know When THERE IS CONFLICT WITH YOUR CO-WORKERS

Honor all people. Love the brotherhood. Fear God. Honor the king.

Servants, be submissive to your masters with all fear, not only to the good and gentle, but also to the harsh. For this is commendable, if because of conscience toward God one endures grief, suffering wrongfully. For what credit is it if, when you are beaten for your faults, you take it patiently? But when you do good and suffer, if you take it patiently, this is commendable before God. For to this you were called, because Christ also suffered for us, leaving us an example, that you should follow His steps:

"Who committed no sin,
Nor was deceit found in His mouth";

who, when He was reviled, did not revile in return; when He suffered, He did not threaten, but committed Himself to Him who judges righteously.

—1 PETER 2:17–23

Bless those who persecute you; bless and do not curse. Rejoice with those who rejoice, and weep with those who weep. Be of the same mind toward one another. Do not set your mind on high things, but associate with the humble. Do not be wise in your own opinion.

Repay no one evil for evil. Have regard for good things in the sight of all men. If it is possible, as much as depends on you, live peaceably with all men. Beloved, do not avenge yourselves, but rather give place to wrath; for it is written, *"Vengeance is Mine, I will repay,"* says the Lord.

—ROMANS 12:14–19

The crown of the wise is their riches,
But the foolishness of fools is folly.

In the fear of the LORD there is strong confidence,
And His children will have a place of refuge.
The fear of the LORD is a fountain of life,
To turn one away from the snares of death.

He who is slow to wrath has great understanding,
But he who is impulsive exalts folly.

—PROVERBS 14:24, 26–27, 29

Now we exhort you, brethren, warn those who are unruly, comfort the fainthearted, uphold the weak, be patient with all. See that no one renders evil for evil to anyone, but always pursue what is good both for yourselves and for all.

Rejoice always, pray without ceasing, in everything give thanks; for this is the will of God in Christ Jesus for you.

—1 Thessalonians 5:14–18

A soft answer turns away wrath,
    But a harsh word stirs up anger.
The tongue of the wise uses knowledge rightly,
    But the mouth of fools pours forth foolishness.

The eyes of the Lord are in every place,
    Keeping watch on the evil and the good.

A wholesome tongue is a tree of life,
    But perverseness in it breaks the spirit.

—Proverbs 15:1–4

Rest in the Lord, and wait patiently for Him;
    Do not fret because of him who prospers
        in his way,

Because of the man who brings wicked
    schemes to pass.
Cease from anger, and forsake wrath;
    Do not fret—it only causes harm.

For evildoers shall be cut off;
    But those who wait on the LORD,
    They shall inherit the earth.

—PSALM 37:7–9

So then, my beloved brethren, let every man
be swift to hear, slow to speak, slow to wrath;
for the wrath of man does not produce the
righteousness of God.
    Therefore lay aside all filthiness and
overflow of wickedness, and receive with
meekness the implanted word, which is able to
save your souls. But be doers of the word, and
not hearers only, deceiving yourselves. For if
anyone is a hearer of the word and not a doer,
he is like a man observing his natural face in a
mirror; for he observes himself, goes away, and
immediately forgets what kind of man he was.
But he who looks into the perfect law of liberty
and continues in it, and is not a forgetful
hearer but a doer of the work, this one will be
blessed in what he does.

—JAMES 1:19–25

What You Should Know When
YOUR FELLOW WORKERS
CRITICIZE YOUR FAITH

"Blessed are you when they revile and persecute you, and say all kinds of evil against you falsely for My sake. Rejoice and be exceedingly glad, for great is your reward in heaven, for so they persecuted the prophets who were before you.

"You are the salt of the earth; but if the salt loses its flavor, how shall it be seasoned? It is then good for nothing but to be thrown out and trampled underfoot by men.

"You are the light of the world. A city that is set on a hill cannot be hidden. Nor do they light a lamp and put it under a basket, but on a lampstand, and it gives light to all who are in the house. Let your light so shine before men, that they may see your good works and glorify your Father in heaven."

"You have heard that it was said, '*You shall love your neighbor* and hate your enemy.' But I say to you, love your enemies, bless those who curse you, do good to those who hate you, and pray for those who spitefully use you and persecute you, that you may be sons of your Father in heaven; for He makes His sun rise on the evil and on the good, and sends rain on the just and on the unjust. For if you love those who love you, what reward have you? Do not even the tax collectors do the same? And if you greet your brethren only, what do you do more than others? Do not even the tax collectors do so? Therefore you shall be perfect, just as your Father in heaven is perfect."

—MATTHEW 5:11–16, 43–48

"God resists the proud,
*   But gives grace to the humble."*

Therefore submit to God. Resist the devil and he will flee from you. Draw near to God and He will draw near to you. Cleanse your hands, you sinners; and purify your hearts, you double-minded. . . . Humble yourselves in the sight of the Lord, and He will lift you up.

—JAMES 4:6B–8, 10

"A good man out of the good treasure of his heart brings forth good things, and an evil man out of the evil treasure brings forth evil things."

—MATTHEW 12:35

Then Jesus said to His disciples, "If anyone desires to come after Me, let him deny himself, and take up his cross, and follow Me. For whoever desires to save his life will lose it, but whoever loses his life for My sake will find it. For what profit is it to a man if he gains the whole world, and loses his own soul? Or what will a man give in exchange for his soul? For the Son of Man will come in the glory of His Father with His angels, and then He will reward each according to his works. Assuredly, I say to you, there are some standing here who shall not taste death till they see the Son of Man coming in His kingdom."

—MATTHEW 16:24–28

Beloved, I beg you as sojourners and pilgrims, abstain from fleshly lusts which war against the soul, having your conduct honorable among the Gentiles, that when they speak against you as evildoers, they may, by your good works which they observe, glorify God in the day of visitation.

Therefore submit yourselves to every ordinance of man for the Lord's sake, whether to the king as supreme, or to governors, as to those who are sent by him for the punishment of evildoers and for the praise of those who do good. For this is the will of God, that by doing good you may put to silence the ignorance of foolish men.

—1 PETER 2:11–15

Beloved, do not think it strange concerning the fiery trial which is to try you, as though some strange thing happened to you; but rejoice to the extent that you partake of Christ's sufferings, that when His glory is revealed, you may also be glad with exceeding joy. If you are reproached for the name of Christ, blessed are you, for the Spirit of glory and of God rests upon you. On their part He is blasphemed, but on your part He is glorified.

—1 PETER 4:12–14

Finally, my brethren, be strong in the Lord and in the power of His might. Put on the whole armor of God, that you may be able to stand against the wiles of the devil. For we do not wrestle against flesh and blood, but against principalities, against powers, against the rulers of the darkness of this age, against spiritual hosts of wickedness in the heavenly places. Therefore take up the whole armor of God, that you may be able to withstand in the evil day, and having done all, to stand. Stand therefore, having girded your waist with truth, having put on the breastplate of righteousness, and having shod your feet with the preparation of the gospel of peace; above all, taking the shield of faith with which you will be able to quench all the fiery darts of the wicked one. And take the helmet of salvation, and the sword of the Spirit, which is the word of God; praying always with all prayer and supplication in the Spirit, being watchful to this end with all perseverance and supplication for all the saints.

—EPHESIANS 6:10–18

What You Should Know When
YOU NEED CONFIDENCE

Do not be afraid of sudden terror,
    Nor of trouble from the wicked when it comes;
For the LORD will be your confidence,
    And will keep your foot from being caught.
    —PROVERBS 3:25–26

Therefore do not cast away your confidence,
which has great reward. For you have need of
endurance, so that after you have done the will
of God, you may receive the promise.
    —HEBREWS 10:35–36

Now this is the confidence that we have in
Him, that if we ask anything according to His
will, He hears us. And if we know that He
hears us, whatever we ask, we know that we
have the petitions that we have asked of Him.
    —1 JOHN 5:14–15

I can do all things through Christ who
strengthens me.
    —PHILIPPIANS 4:13

My little children, let us not love in word or in tongue, but in deed and in truth. And by this we know that we are of the truth, and shall assure our hearts before Him. For if our heart condemns us, God is greater than our heart, and knows all things.

Beloved, if our heart does not condemn us, we have confidence toward God. And whatever we ask we receive from Him, because we keep His commandments and do those things that are pleasing in His sight. And this is His commandment: that we should believe on the name of His Son Jesus Christ and love one another, as He gave us commandment. Now he who keeps His commandments abides in Him, and He in him. And by this we know that He abides in us, by the Spirit whom He has given us.

—1 JOHN 3:18–24

"Most assuredly, I say to you, he who believes in Me, the works that I do he will do also; and greater works than these he will do, because I go to My Father. And whatever you ask in My name, that I will do, that the Father may be glorified in the Son. If you ask anything in My name, I will do it. If you love Me, keep My commandments. And I will pray the Father, and He will give you another Helper, that He may abide with you forever."

—JOHN 14:12–16

Who shall separate us from the love of Christ? Shall tribulation, or distress, or persecution, or famine, or nakedness, or peril, or sword? As it is written:

"For Your sake we are killed all day long;
We are accounted as sheep for the slaughter."

Yet in all these things we are more than conquerors through Him who loved us. For I am persuaded that neither death nor life, nor angels nor principalities nor powers, nor things present nor things to come, nor height nor depth, nor any other created thing, shall be able to separate us from the love of God which is in Christ Jesus our Lord.

—ROMANS 8:35–39

What to Do When . . .

Give instruction to a wise man, and he
      will be still wiser;
    Teach a just man, and he will increase
      in learning.
"The fear of the LORD is the beginning
      of wisdom,
    And the knowledge of the Holy One is
      understanding.
For by me your days will be multiplied,
    And years of life will be added to you.
If you are wise, you are wise for yourself,
    And if you scoff, you will bear it alone."

            —PROVERBS 9:9–12

What to Do When
YOU ARE ASKED TO DO
SOMETHING UNETHICAL

Do not be envious of evil men,
   Nor desire to be with them;
For their heart devises violence,
   And their lips talk of troublemaking.

Through wisdom a house is built,
   And by understanding it is established;
By knowledge the rooms are filled
   With all precious and pleasant riches.

A wise man is strong,
   Yes, a man of knowledge increases strength;
For by wise counsel you will wage your own war,
   And in a multitude of counselors there
      is safety.

—PROVERBS 24:1–6

LORD, I have loved the habitation of Your house,
   And the place where Your glory dwells.

Do not gather my soul with sinners,
   Nor my life with bloodthirsty men,

In whose hands is a sinister scheme,
    And whose right hand is full of bribes.

But as for me, I will walk in my integrity;
    Redeem me and be merciful to me.
My foot stands in an even place;
    In the congregations I will bless the LORD.

                                        —PSALM 26:8–12

My son, if sinners entice you,
    Do not consent.
If they say, "Come with us,
    Let us lie in wait to shed blood;
    Let us lurk secretly for the innocent without
        cause;
Let us swallow them alive like Sheol,
    And whole, like those who go down to the Pit;
We shall find all kinds of precious possessions,
    We shall fill our houses with spoil;
Cast in your lot among us,
    Let us all have one purse"—
My son, do not walk in the way with them,
    Keep your foot from their path;
For their feet run to evil,
    And they make haste to shed blood.
Surely, in vain the net is spread

In the sight of any bird;
But they lie in wait for their own blood,
They lurk secretly for their own lives.
So are the ways of everyone who is greedy
        for gain;
It takes away the life of its owners.

—PROVERBS 1:10–19

Let no one deceive you with empty words,
for because of these things the wrath of God
comes upon the sons of disobedience.
Therefore do not be partakers with them.

For you were once darkness, but now you
are light in the Lord. Walk as children of light
(for the fruit of the Spirit is in all goodness,
righteousness, and truth), finding out what is
acceptable to the Lord. And have no fellowship
with the unfruitful works of darkness, but
rather expose them. For it is shameful even to
speak of those things which are done by them
in secret.

—EPHESIANS 5:6–12

My son, if your heart is wise,
My heart will rejoice—indeed, I myself;
Yes, my inmost being will rejoice
When your lips speak right things.

Do not let your heart envy sinners,
But be zealous for the fear of the LORD all
the day;
For surely there is a hereafter,
And your hope will not be cut off.

—PROVERBS 23:15–18

Do not love the world or the things in the world. If anyone loves the world, the love of the Father is not in him. For all that is in the world—the lust of the flesh, the lust of the eyes, and the pride of life—is not of the Father but is of the world. And the world is passing away, and the lust of it; but he who does the will of God abides forever.

—1 JOHN 2:15–17

What to Do When
You Are
Faced with a Crisis

Because you have made the LORD, who is my
        refuge,
    Even the Most High, your dwelling place,
No evil shall befall you,
    Nor shall any plague come near your dwelling;
For He shall give His angels charge over you,
    To keep you in all your ways.
In their hands they shall bear you up,
    Lest you dash your foot against a stone.
You shall tread upon the lion and the cobra,
    The young lion and the serpent you shall
        trample underfoot.

"Because he has set his love upon Me,
        therefore I will deliver him;
    I will set him on high, because he has
        known My name.
He shall call upon Me, and I will answer him;
    I will be with him in trouble;
    I will deliver him and honor him.
With long life I will satisfy him,
    And show him My salvation."

—PSALM 91:9–16

As for me, I will call upon God,
    And the LORD shall save me.
Evening and morning and at noon
    I will pray, and cry aloud,
    And He shall hear my voice.
He has redeemed my soul in peace from the
        battle that was against me,
    For there were many against me.

Cast your burden on the LORD,
    And He shall sustain you;
    He shall never permit the righteous to be
        moved.

—PSALM 55:16–18, 22

The LORD upholds all who fall,
    And raises up all who are bowed down.

The LORD is righteous in all His ways,
    Gracious in all His works.
The LORD is near to all who call upon Him,
    To all who call upon Him in truth.
He will fulfill the desire of those who fear Him;
    He also will hear their cry and save them.
The LORD preserves all who love Him,
    But all the wicked He will destroy.

—PSALM 145:14, 17–20

Give ear, O LORD, to my prayer;
    And attend to the voice of my supplications.
In the day of my trouble I will call upon You,
    For You will answer me.

Among the gods there is none like You, O Lord;
    Nor are there any works like Your works.
All nations whom You have made
    Shall come and worship before You, O Lord,
    And shall glorify Your name.

For You are great, and do wondrous things;
    You alone are God.

—PSALM 86:6–10

I sought the LORD, and He heard me,
    And delivered me from all my fears.
They looked to Him and were radiant,
    And their faces were not ashamed.
This poor man cried out, and the LORD heard him,
    And saved him out of all his troubles.
The angel of the LORD encamps all around
            those who fear Him,
    And delivers them.

Oh, taste and see that the LORD is good;
    Blessed is the man who trusts in Him!

—PSALM 34:4–8

Though the LORD is on high,
Yet He regards the lowly;
But the proud He knows from afar.

Though I walk in the midst of trouble,
You will revive me;
You will stretch out Your hand
Against the wrath of my enemies,
And Your right hand will save me.
The LORD will perfect that which concerns me;
Your mercy, O LORD, endures forever;
Do not forsake the works of Your hands.

—PSALM 138:6–8

Casting all your care upon Him, for He cares for you.

Be sober, be vigilant; because your adversary the devil walks about like a roaring lion, seeking whom he may devour. Resist him, steadfast in the faith, knowing that the same sufferings are experienced by your brotherhood in the world.

But may the God of all grace, who called us to His eternal glory by Christ Jesus, after you have suffered a while, perfect, establish, strengthen, and settle you.

—1 PETER 5:7–10

But now, thus says the LORD, who created you,
    O Jacob,
  And He who formed you, O Israel:
  "Fear not, for I have redeemed you;
  I have called you by your name;
  You are Mine.
When you pass through the waters,
    I will be with you;
  And through the rivers, they shall not
    overflow you.
  When you walk through the fire, you shall
    not be burned,
  Nor shall the flame scorch you.
For I am the LORD your God,
  The Holy One of Israel, your Savior.

—ISAIAH 43:1–3A

What to Do When
SOMEONE TELLS
A LIE ABOUT YOU

The proud have forged a lie against me,
    But I will keep Your precepts with my
        whole heart.
Their heart is as fat as grease,
    But I delight in Your law.
It is good for me that I have been afflicted,
    That I may learn Your statutes.
The law of Your mouth is better to me
    Than thousands of coins of gold and silver.

—PSALM 119:69–72

A false witness will not go unpunished,
    And he who speaks lies will not escape.

He who gets wisdom loves his own soul;
    He who keeps understanding will find good.

A false witness will not go unpunished,
    And he who speaks lies shall perish.

—PROVERBS 19:5, 8–9

How long will you attack a man?
    You shall be slain, all of you,
    Like a leaning wall and a tottering fence.
They only consult to cast him down from
        his high position;
    They delight in lies;
    They bless with their mouth,
    But they curse inwardly.

My soul, wait silently for God alone,
    For my expectation is from Him.
He only is my rock and my salvation;
    He is my defense;
    I shall not be moved.
In God is my salvation and my glory;
    The rock of my strength,
    And my refuge, is in God.

—Psalm 62:3–7

Whoever secretly slanders his neighbor,
    Him I will destroy;
    The one who has a haughty look and a
        proud heart,
    Him I will not endure.

My eyes shall be on the faithful of the land,

That they may dwell with me;
He who walks in a perfect way,
He shall serve me.

He who works deceit shall not dwell within
my house;
He who tells lies shall not continue in
my presence.
Early I will destroy all the wicked of the land,
That I may cut off all the evildoers from
the city of the LORD.

—PSALM 101:5–8

A man who bears false witness against his
neighbor
Is like a club, a sword, and a sharp arrow.

Confidence in an unfaithful man in time
of trouble
Is like a bad tooth and a foot out of joint.

Like one who takes away a garment in
cold weather,
And like vinegar on soda,
Is one who sings songs to a heavy heart.

—PROVERBS 25:18–20

He who speaks truth declares righteousness,
    But a false witness, deceit.
There is one who speaks like the piercings
        of a sword,
    But the tongue of the wise promotes health.
The truthful lip shall be established forever,
    But a lying tongue is but for a moment.
Deceit is in the heart of those who devise evil,
    But counselors of peace have joy.
No grave trouble will overtake the righteous,
    But the wicked shall be filled with evil.
Lying lips are an abomination to the LORD,
    But those who deal truthfully are His delight.

                —PROVERBS 12:17–22

These six things the LORD hates,
    Yes, seven are an abomination to Him:
A proud look,
    A lying tongue,
    Hands that shed innocent blood,
A heart that devises wicked plans,
    Feet that are swift in running to evil,
A false witness who speaks lies,
    And one who sows discord among brethren.

My son, keep your father's command,

And do not forsake the law of your mother.
Bind them continually upon your heart;
Tie them around your neck.
When you roam, they will lead you;
When you sleep, they will keep you;
And when you awake, they will speak with you.
For the commandment is a lamp,
And the law a light;
Reproofs of instruction are the way of life.

—PROVERBS 6:16–23

What to Do When
YOU HAVE COMPROMISED
YOUR INTEGRITY

If You, LORD, should mark iniquities,
O Lord, who could stand?
But there is forgiveness with You,
That You may be feared.

I wait for the LORD, my soul waits,
And in His word I do hope.

—PSALM 130:3—5

Not that I have already attained, or am already perfected; but I press on, that I may lay hold of that for which Christ Jesus has also laid hold of me. Brethren, I do not count myself to have apprehended; but one thing I do, forgetting those things which are behind and reaching forward to those things which are ahead, I press toward the goal for the prize of the upward call of God in Christ Jesus.

—PHILIPPIANS 3:12—14

For what I am doing, I do not understand. For what I will to do, that I do not practice; but what I hate, that I do. If, then, I do what I will not to do, I agree with the law that it is good. But now, it is no longer I who do it, but sin that dwells in me. For I know that in me (that is, in my flesh) nothing good dwells; for to will is present with me, but how to perform what is good I do not find. For the good that I will to do, I do not do; but the evil I will not to do, that I practice. Now if I do what I will not to do, it is no longer I who do it, but sin that dwells in me.

I find then a law, that evil is present with me, the one who wills to do good. For I delight in the law of God according to the inward man. But I see another law in my members, warring against the law of my mind, and bringing me into captivity to the law of sin which is in my members. O wretched man that I am! Who will deliver me from this body of death? I thank God—through Jesus Christ our Lord! So then, with the mind I myself serve the law of God, but with the flesh the law of sin.

There is therefore now no condemnation to those who are in Christ Jesus, who do not walk according to the flesh, but according to the Spirit. For the law of the Spirit of life in Christ Jesus has made me free from the law of sin and death.

—ROMANS 7:15–8:2

If we say that we have fellowship with Him, and walk in darkness, we lie and do not practice the truth. But if we walk in the light as He is in the light, we have fellowship with one another, and the blood of Jesus Christ His Son cleanses us from all sin.

If we say that we have no sin, we deceive ourselves, and the truth is not in us. If we confess our sins, He is faithful and just to forgive us our sins and to cleanse us from all unrighteousness.

—I JOHN 1:6–9

Purge me with hyssop, and I shall be clean;
    Wash me, and I shall be whiter than snow.
Make me hear joy and gladness,
    That the bones You have broken may rejoice.

Hide Your face from my sins,
And blot out all my iniquities.

Create in me a clean heart, O God,
And renew a steadfast spirit within me.
Do not cast me away from Your presence,
And do not take Your Holy Spirit from me.

Restore to me the joy of Your salvation,
And uphold me by Your generous Spirit.

—PSALM 51:7–12

Be merciful to me, O Lord,
For I cry to You all day long.
Rejoice the soul of Your servant,
For to You, O Lord, I lift up my soul.
For You, Lord, are good; and ready to forgive,
And abundant in mercy to all those who
call upon You.

—PSALM 86:3–5

What to Do When
YOU NEED TO SEEK FORGIVENESS
FROM A FELLOW WORKER

If we say that we have no sin, we deceive ourselves, and the truth is not in us. If we confess our sins, He is faithful and just to forgive us our sins and to cleanse us from all unrighteousness. If we say that we have not sinned, we make Him a liar, and His word is not in us.

—1 JOHN 1:8–10

Now He who searches the hearts knows what the mind of the Spirit is, because He makes intercession for the saints according to the will of God. And we know that all things work together for good to those who love God, to those who are the called according to His purpose.

—ROMANS 8:27–28

As many as I love, I rebuke and chasten. Therefore be zealous and repent.

—REVELATION 3:19

Bless the LORD, O my soul;
   And all that is within me, bless His holy name!
Bless the LORD, O my soul,
   And forget not all His benefits:
Who forgives all your iniquities,
   Who heals all your diseases,
Who redeems your life from destruction,
      Who crowns you with lovingkindness and
            tender mercies,
Who satisfies your mouth with good things,
   So that your youth is renewed like the eagle's.

—PSALM 103:1–5

   Confess your trespasses to one another, and
pray for one another, that you may be healed.
The effective, fervent prayer of a righteous
man avails much.

—JAMES 5:16

What to Do When
YOUR FRIENDS AND NEIGHBORS
ARE IN TOTAL DARKNESS

"You are the light of the world. A city that is set on a hill cannot be hidden. Nor do they light a lamp and put it under a basket, but on a lampstand, and it gives light to all who are in the house. Let your light so shine before men, that they may see your good works and glorify your Father in heaven."

—MATTHEW 5:14–16

But you, brethren, are not in darkness, so that this Day should overtake you as a thief. You are all sons of light and sons of the day. We are not of the night nor of darkness. Therefore let us not sleep, as others do, but let us watch and be sober. For those who sleep, sleep at night, and those who get drunk are drunk at night. But let us who are of the day be sober, putting on the breastplate of faith and love, and as a helmet the hope of salvation. For God did not appoint us to wrath, but to obtain salvation through our Lord Jesus Christ.

—1 THESSALONIANS 5:4–9

Then Jesus said to them, "A little while longer the light is with you. Walk while you have the light, lest darkness overtake you; he who walks in darkness does not know where he is going. While you have the light, believe in the light, that you may become sons of light." These things Jesus spoke, and departed, and was hidden from them.

—JOHN 12:35–36

"For God so loved the world that He gave His only begotten Son, that whoever believes in Him should not perish but have everlasting life. For God did not send His Son into the world to condemn the world, but that the world through Him might be saved."

—JOHN 3:16–17

If you confess with your mouth the Lord Jesus and believe in your heart that God has raised Him from the dead, you will be saved. For with the heart one believes unto righteousness, and with the mouth confession is made unto salvation.

—ROMANS 10:9–10

Then Jesus spoke to them again, saying, "I am the light of the world. He who follows Me shall not walk in darkness, but have the light of life."

—JOHN 8:12

But sanctify the Lord God in your hearts, and always be ready to give a defense to everyone who asks you a reason for the hope that is in you, with meekness and fear.

—1 PETER 3:15

But, beloved, do not forget this one thing, that with the Lord one day is as a thousand years, and a thousand years as one day. The Lord is not slack concerning His promise, as some count slackness, but is longsuffering toward us, not willing that any should perish but that all should come to repentance.

—2 PETER 3:8–9

What to Do When
A FRIEND NEEDS
YOUR ENCOURAGEMENT

Blessed be the God and Father of our Lord Jesus Christ, the Father of mercies and God of all comfort, who comforts us in all our tribulation, that we may be able to comfort those who are in any trouble, with the comfort with which we ourselves are comforted by God.

—2 CORINTHIANS 1:3–4

Therefore comfort each other and edify one another, just as you also are doing.

And we urge you, brethren, to recognize those who labor among you, and are over you in the Lord and admonish you, and to esteem them very highly in love for their work's sake. Be at peace among yourselves.

—1 THESSALONIANS 5:11–13

For the kingdom of God is not eating and drinking, but righteousness and peace and joy in the Holy Spirit. For he who serves Christ in these things is acceptable to God and approved by men. Therefore let us pursue the things which make for peace and the things by which one may edify another.

—ROMANS 14:17–19

Let love be without hypocrisy. Abhor what is evil. Cling to what is good. Be kindly affectionate to one another with brotherly love, in honor giving preference to one another; not lagging in diligence, fervent in spirit, serving the Lord; rejoicing in hope, patient in tribulation, continuing steadfastly in prayer; distributing to the needs of the saints, given to hospitality.

—ROMANS 12:9–13

I, therefore, the prisoner of the Lord, beseech you to walk worthy of the calling with which you were called, with all lowliness and gentleness, with longsuffering, bearing with one another in love, endeavoring to keep the unity of the Spirit in the bond of peace. There is one body and one Spirit, just as you were called in one hope of your calling; one Lord, one faith, one baptism; one God and Father of all, who is above all, and through all, and in you all.

But to each one of us grace was given according to the measure of Christ's gift.

—EPHESIANS 4:1–7

Therefore, as the elect of God, holy and beloved, put on tender mercies, kindness, humility, meekness, longsuffering; bearing with one another, and forgiving one another, if anyone has a complaint against another; even as Christ forgave you, so you also must do. But above all these things put on love, which is the bond of perfection.

And let the peace of God rule in your hearts, to which also you were called in one body; and be thankful. Let the word of Christ dwell in you richly in all wisdom, teaching and admonishing one another in psalms and hymns and spiritual songs, singing with grace in your hearts to the Lord. And whatever you do in word or deed, do all in the name of the Lord Jesus, giving thanks to God the Father through Him.

—COLOSSIANS 3:12–17

For you, brethren, have been called to liberty; only do not use liberty as an opportunity for the flesh, but through love serve one another. For all the law is fulfilled in one word, even in this: *"You shall love your neighbor as yourself."*

—GALATIANS 5:13–14

Therefore if there is any consolation in Christ, if any comfort of love, if any fellowship of the Spirit, if any affection and mercy, fulfill my joy by being like-minded, having the same love, being of one accord, of one mind. Let nothing be done through selfish ambition or conceit, but in lowliness of mind let each esteem others better than himself. Let each of you look out not only for his own interests, but also for the interests of others.

Let this mind be in you which was also in Christ Jesus.

—PHILIPPIANS 2:1–5

What the Bible Says About . . .

The LORD by wisdom founded the earth;
  By understanding He established
    the heavens;
By His knowledge the depths were
    broken up,
  And clouds drop down the dew.

My son, let them not depart from
    your eyes—
  Keep sound wisdom and discretion;
So they will be life to your soul
  And grace to your neck.
Then you will walk safely in your way,
  And your foot will not stumble.

—PROVERBS 3:19–23

What the Bible Says About
SEXUAL TEMPTATION

Therefore let him who thinks he stands take heed lest he fall. No temptation has overtaken you except such as is common to man; but God is faithful, who will not allow you to be tempted beyond what you are able, but with the temptation will also make the way of escape, that you may be able to bear it.

—1 CORINTHIANS 10:12–13

I say then: Walk in the Spirit, and you shall not fulfill the lust of the flesh. For the flesh lusts against the Spirit, and the Spirit against the flesh; and these are contrary to one another, so that you do not do the things that you wish. But if you are led by the Spirit, you are not under the law.

Now the works of the flesh are evident, which are: adultery, fornication, uncleanness, lewdness.

—GALATIANS 5:16–19

All things are lawful for me, but all things are not helpful. All things are lawful for me, but I will not be brought under the power of any. Foods for the stomach and the stomach for foods, but God will destroy both it and them. Now the body is not for sexual immorality but for the Lord, and the Lord for the body. And God both raised up the Lord and will also raise us up by His power. Do you not know that your bodies are members of Christ? Shall I then take the members of Christ and make them members of a harlot? Certainly not! Or do you not know that he who is joined to a harlot is one body with her? For *"the two,"* He says, *"shall become one flesh."* But he who is joined to the Lord is one spirit with Him.

Flee sexual immorality. Every sin that a man does is outside the body, but he who commits sexual immorality sins against his own body. Or do you not know that your body is the temple of the Holy Spirit who is in you, whom you have from God, and you are not your own? For you were bought at a price; therefore glorify God in your body and in your spirit, which are God's.

—1 CORINTHIANS 6:12–20

Blessed is the man who endures temptation;
for when he has been approved, he will receive
the crown of life which the Lord has promised
to those who love Him.

Let no one say when he is tempted, "I am
tempted by God"; for God cannot be tempted
by evil, nor does He Himself tempt anyone. But
each one is tempted when he is drawn away by
his own desires and enticed. Then, when desire
has conceived, it gives birth to sin; and sin,
when it is full-grown, brings forth death.

Do not be deceived, my beloved brethren.
Every good gift and every perfect gift is from
above, and comes down from the Father of
lights, with whom there is no variation or
shadow of turning.

—JAMES 1:12–17

Drink water from your own cistern,
   And running water from your own well.
Should your fountains be dispersed abroad,
   Streams of water in the streets?
Let them be only your own,
   And not for strangers with you.
Let your fountain be blessed,

And rejoice with the wife of your youth.
As a loving deer and a graceful doe,
    Let her breasts satisfy you at all times;
And always be enraptured with her love.
    For why should you, my son, be enraptured
        by an immoral woman,
And be embraced in the arms of a seductress?

For the ways of man are before the eyes of
    the LORD,
    And He ponders all his paths.

—PROVERBS 5:15–21

Whoever commits adultery with a woman
    lacks understanding;
    He who does so destroys his own soul.
Wounds and dishonor he will get,
    And his reproach will not be wiped away.
For jealousy is a husband's fury;
    Therefore he will not spare in the day
        of vengeance.
He will accept no recompense,
    Nor will he be appeased though you give
        many gifts.

—PROVERBS 6:32–35

My son, keep my words,
    And treasure my commands within you.
Keep my commands and live,
    And my law as the apple of your eye.
Bind them on your fingers;
    Write them on the tablet of your heart.
Say to wisdom, "You are my sister,"
    And call understanding your nearest kin,
That they may keep you from the immoral
        woman,
    From the seductress who flatters with her
        words.

For at the window of my house
    I looked through my lattice,
And saw among the simple,
    I perceived among the youths,
    A young man devoid of understanding,
Passing along the street near her corner;
    And he took the path to her house
In the twilight, in the evening,
    In the black and dark night.

And there a woman met him,
    With the attire of a harlot, and a crafty heart.
She was loud and rebellious,
    Her feet would not stay at home.

At times she was outside, at times in the
open square,
Lurking at every corner.
So she caught him and kissed him;
With an impudent face she said to him:
"I have peace offerings with me;
Today I have paid my vows.
So I came out to meet you,
Diligently to seek your face,
And I have found you.
I have spread my bed with tapestry,
Colored coverings of Egyptian linen.
I have perfumed my bed
With myrrh, aloes, and cinnamon.
Come, let us take our fill of love until morning;
Let us delight ourselves with love.
For my husband is not at home;
He has gone on a long journey;
He has taken a bag of money with him,
And will come home on the appointed day."

With her enticing speech she caused him
to yield,
With her flattering lips she seduced him.
Immediately he went after her, as an ox goes
to the slaughter,

Or as a fool to the correction of the stocks,
Till an arrow struck his liver.
As a bird hastens to the snare,
He did not know it would cost his life.

Now therefore, listen to me, my children;
Pay attention to the words of my mouth:
Do not let your heart turn aside to her ways,
Do not stray into her paths;
For she has cast down many wounded,
And all who were slain by her were
strong men.
Her house is the way to hell,
Descending to the chambers of death.

—PROVERBS 7

What the Bible Says About
GOSSIP

He who is devoid of wisdom despises his
    neighbor,
    But a man of understanding holds his peace.

A talebearer reveals secrets,
    But he who is of a faithful spirit conceals
       a matter.

Where there is no counsel, the people fall;
    But in the multitude of counselors there
       is safety.

—PROVERBS 11:12–14

Where there is no wood, the fire goes out;
    And where there is no talebearer, strife ceases.
As charcoal is to burning coals, and wood
       to fire,
    So is a contentious man to kindle strife.
The words of a talebearer are like tasty trifles,
    And they go down into the inmost body.

—PROVERBS 26:20–22

He who goes about as a talebearer reveals secrets;
   Therefore do not associate with one who
      flatters with his lips.

—PROVERBS 20:19

He who keeps instruction is in the way of life,
   But he who refuses correction goes astray.

Whoever hides hatred has lying lips,
   And whoever spreads slander is a fool.

In the multitude of words sin is not lacking,
   But he who restrains his lips is wise.
The tongue of the righteous is choice silver;
   The heart of the wicked is worth little.
The lips of the righteous feed many,
   But fools die for lack of wisdom.

—PROVERBS 10:17–21

A wise son heeds his father's instruction,
   But a scoffer does not listen to rebuke.

A man shall eat well by the fruit of his mouth,
   But the soul of the unfaithful feeds on violence.
He who guards his mouth preserves his life,
   But he who opens wide his lips shall have
      destruction.

—PROVERBS 13:1–3

My brethren, let not many of you become teachers, knowing that we shall receive a stricter judgment. For we all stumble in many things. If anyone does not stumble in word, he is a perfect man, able also to bridle the whole body.

Indeed, we put bits in horses' mouths that they may obey us, and we turn their whole body. Look also at ships: although they are so large and are driven by fierce winds, they are turned by a very small rudder wherever the pilot desires. Even so the tongue is a little member and boasts great things. See how great a forest a little fire kindles! And the tongue is a fire, a world of iniquity. The tongue is so set among our members that it defiles the whole body, and sets on fire the course of nature; and it is set on fire by hell. . . .

With it we bless our God and Father, and with it we curse men, who have been made in the similitude of God. Out of the same mouth proceed blessing and cursing. My brethren, these things ought not to be so. . . .

Who is wise and understanding among you? Let him show by good conduct that his works are done in the meekness of wisdom.

—JAMES 3:1–6, 9–10, 13

A soft answer turns away wrath,
But a harsh word stirs up anger.
The tongue of the wise uses knowledge rightly,
But the mouth of fools pours forth foolishness.

The eyes of the LORD are in every place,
Keeping watch on the evil and the good.

A wholesome tongue is a tree of life,
But perverseness in it breaks the spirit.

A fool despises his father's instruction,
But he who receives correction is prudent.

—PROVERBS 15:1–5

Lying lips are an abomination to the LORD,
But those who deal truthfully are His delight.

—PROVERBS 12:22

What the Bible Says About
LOYALTY

What does it profit, my brethren, if someone says he has faith but does not have works? Can faith save him? If a brother or sister is naked and destitute of daily food, and one of you says to them, "Depart in peace, be warmed and filled," but you do not give them the things which are needed for the body, what does it profit? Thus also faith by itself, if it does not have works, is dead.

But someone will say, "You have faith, and I have works." Show me your faith without your works, and I will show you my faith by my works.

—JAMES 2:14–18

"When the Son of Man comes in His glory, and all the holy angels with Him, then He will sit on the throne of His glory. All the nations will be gathered before Him, and He will separate them one from another, as a shepherd divides his sheep from the goats. And He will set the sheep on His right hand, but the goats on the left.

"Then the King will say to those on His right hand, 'Come, you blessed of My Father, inherit the kingdom prepared for you from the foundation of the world: for I was hungry and you gave Me food; I was thirsty and you gave Me drink; I was a stranger and you took Me in; I was naked and you clothed Me; I was sick and you visited Me; I was in prison and you came to Me.'

"Then the righteous will answer Him, saying, 'Lord, when did we see You hungry and feed You, or thirsty and give You drink? When did we see You a stranger and take You in, or naked and clothe You? Or when did we see You sick, or in prison, and come to You?'

"And the King will answer and say to them, 'Assuredly, I say to you, inasmuch as you did it to one of the least of these My brethren, you did it to Me.'"

—MATTHEW 25:31–40

"A new commandment I give to you, that you love one another; as I have loved you, that you also love one another. By this all will know that you are My disciples, if you have love for one another."

—JOHN 13:34–35

"But lay up for yourselves treasures in heaven, where neither moth nor rust destroys and where thieves do not break in and steal. For where your treasure is, there your heart will be also.

"The lamp of the body is the eye. If therefore your eye is good, your whole body will be full of light. But if your eye is bad, your whole body will be full of darkness. If therefore the light that is in you is darkness, how great is that darkness!

"But seek first the kingdom of God and His righteousness, and all these things shall be added to you."

—MATTHEW 6:20–23, 33

A good man deals graciously and lends;
    He will guide his affairs with discretion.
Surely he will never be shaken;
    The righteous will be in everlasting
        remembrance.
He will not be afraid of evil tidings;
    His heart is steadfast, trusting in the LORD.

—PSALM 112:5–7

What the Bible Says About
SERVING GOD

"You shall walk after the LORD your God and fear Him, and keep His commandments and obey His voice; you shall serve Him and hold fast to Him."

—DEUTERONOMY 13:4

"No one can serve two masters; for either he will hate the one and love the other, or else he will be loyal to the one and despise the other. You cannot serve God and mammon."

—MATTHEW 6:24

"But take careful heed to do the commandment and the law which Moses the servant of the LORD commanded you, to love the LORD your God, to walk in all His ways, to keep His commandments, to hold fast to Him, and to serve Him with all your heart and with all your soul."

—JOSHUA 22:5

I beseech you therefore, brethren, by the mercies of God, that you present your bodies a living sacrifice, holy, acceptable to God, which is your reasonable service. And do not be conformed to this world, but be transformed by the renewing of your mind, that you may prove what is that good and acceptable and perfect will of God.

—ROMANS 12:1–2

Be kindly affectionate to one another with brotherly love, in honor giving preference to one another; not lagging in diligence, fervent in spirit, serving the Lord; . . . distributing to the needs of the saints, given to hospitality.

—ROMANS 12:10–11, 13

"And now, Israel, what does the LORD your God require of you, but to fear the LORD your God, to walk in all His ways and to love Him, to serve the LORD your God with all your heart and with all your soul."

—DEUTERONOMY 10:12

"And it shall be that if you earnestly obey My commandments which I command you today, to love the LORD your God and serve Him with all your heart and with all your soul, then I will give you the rain for your land in its season, the early rain and the latter rain, that you may gather in your grain, your new wine, and your oil. And I will send grass in your fields for your livestock, that you may eat and be filled."

—DEUTERONOMY 11:13–15

Make a joyful shout to the LORD, all you lands!
Serve the LORD with gladness;
    Come before His presence with singing.

Enter into His gates with thanksgiving,
    And into His courts with praise.
    Be thankful to Him, and bless His name.

—PSALM 100:1–2, 4

"So you shall serve the LORD your God, and He will bless your bread and your water. And I will take sickness away from the midst of you. No one shall suffer miscarriage or be barren in your land; I will fulfill the number of your days."

—EXODUS 23:25–26

What the Bible Says About
ETERNITY

And this is the testimony: that God has given us eternal life, and this life is in His Son. He who has the Son has life; he who does not have the Son of God does not have life.

These things I have written to you who believe in the name of the Son of God, that you may know that you have eternal life, and that you may *continue to* believe in the name of the Son of God.

—1 JOHN 5:11–13

"Most assuredly, I say to you, he who believes in Me has everlasting life. I am the bread of life. Your fathers ate the manna in the wilderness, and are dead. This is the bread which comes down from heaven, that one may eat of it and not die. I am the living bread which came down from heaven. If anyone eats of this bread, he will live forever; and the bread that I shall give is My flesh, which I shall give for the life of the world."

—JOHN 6:47–51

"For God so loved the world that He gave His only begotten Son, that whoever believes in Him should not perish but have everlasting life. For God did not send His Son into the world to condemn the world, but that the world through Him might be saved."

—JOHN 3:16–17

We know that we are of God, and the whole world lies under the sway of the wicked one. And we know that the Son of God has come and has given us an understanding, that we may know Him who is true; and we are in Him who is true, in His Son Jesus Christ. This is the true God and eternal life.

—1 JOHN 5:19–20

"My sheep hear My voice, and I know them, and they follow Me. And I give them eternal life, and they shall never perish; neither shall anyone snatch them out of My hand. My Father, who has given them to Me, is greater than all; and no one is able to snatch them out of My Father's hand. I and My Father are one."

—JOHN 10:27–30

"Most assuredly, I say to you, he who hears My word and believes in Him who sent Me has everlasting life, and shall not come into judgment, but has passed from death into life."

—JOHN 5:24

Jesus answered and said to her, "Whoever drinks of this water will thirst again, but whoever drinks of the water that I shall give him will never thirst. But the water that I shall give him will become in him a fountain of water springing up into everlasting life."

—JOHN 4:13–14

What the Bible Says About
OBEDIENCE

"Behold, I set before you today a blessing and a curse: the blessing, if you obey the commandments of the LORD your God which I command you today; and the curse, if you do not obey the commandments of the LORD your God, but turn aside from the way which I command you today, to go after other gods which you have not known."

—DEUTERONOMY 11:26–28

Now by this we know that we know Him, if we keep His commandments. He who says, "I know Him," and does not keep His commandments, is a liar, and the truth is not in him. But whoever keeps His word, truly the love of God is perfected in him. By this we know that we are in Him. He who says he abides in Him ought himself also to walk just as He walked.

—1 JOHN 2:3–6

"If you love Me, keep My commandments. And I will pray the Father, and He will give you another Helper, that He may abide with you forever—the Spirit of truth, whom the world cannot receive, because it neither sees Him nor knows Him; but you know Him, for He dwells with you and will be in you. I will not leave you orphans; I will come to you. A little while longer and the world will see Me no more, but you will see Me. Because I live, you will live also. At that day you will know that I am in My Father, and you in Me, and I in you. He who has My commandments and keeps them, it is he who loves Me. And he who loves Me will be loved by My Father, and I will love him and manifest Myself to him."

—JOHN 14:15–21

Bondservants, be obedient to those who are your masters according to the flesh, with fear and trembling, in sincerity of heart, as to Christ; not with eyeservice, as men-pleasers, but as bondservants of Christ, doing the will of God from the heart, with goodwill doing service, as to the Lord, and not to men.

—EPHESIANS 6:5–7

And Moses called all Israel, and said to them: "Hear, O Israel, the statutes and judgments which I speak in your hearing today, that you may learn them and be careful to observe them."

"Therefore you shall be careful to do as the LORD your God has commanded you; you shall not turn aside to the right hand or to the left. You shall walk in all the ways which the LORD your God has commanded you, that you may live and that it may be well with you, and that you may prolong your days in the land which you shall possess."

—DEUTERONOMY 5:1, 32–33

Children, obey your parents in all things, for this is well pleasing to the Lord.

Fathers, do not provoke your children, lest they become discouraged.

Bondservants, obey in all things your masters according to the flesh, not with eyeservice, as men-pleasers, but in sincerity of heart, fearing God. And whatever you do, do it heartily, as to the Lord and not to men, knowing that from the Lord you will receive the reward of the inheritance; for you serve the Lord Christ.

—COLOSSIANS 3:20–24

Therefore submit yourselves to every ordinance of man for the Lord's sake, whether to the king as supreme, or to governors, as to those who are sent by him for the punishment of evildoers and for the praise of those who do good. For this is the will of God, that by doing good you may put to silence the ignorance of foolish men—as free, yet not using liberty as a cloak for vice, but as bondservants of God. Honor all people. Love the brotherhood. Fear God. Honor the king.

Servants, be submissive to your masters with all fear, not only to the good and gentle, but also to the harsh. For this is commendable, if because of conscience toward God one endures grief, suffering wrongfully. For what credit is it if, when you are beaten for your faults, you take it patiently? But when you do good and suffer, if you take it patiently, this is commendable before God.

—1 PETER 2:13–20

What the Bible Says About
THE GRACE OF GOD

For the Lord God is a sun and shield;
   The Lord will give grace and glory;
   No good thing will He withhold
   From those who walk uprightly.

—PSALM 84:11

For we do not have a High Priest who cannot sympathize with our weaknesses, but was in all points tempted as we are, yet without sin. Let us therefore come boldly to the throne of grace, that we may obtain mercy and find grace to help in time of need.

—HEBREWS 4:15–16

But God, who is rich in mercy, because of His great love with which He loved us, even when we were dead in trespasses, made us alive together with Christ (by grace you have been saved), and raised us up together, and made us sit together in the heavenly places in Christ

Jesus, that in the ages to come He might show the exceeding riches of His grace in His kindness toward us in Christ Jesus. For by grace you have been saved through faith, and that not of yourselves; it is the gift of God, not of works, lest anyone should boast. For we are His workmanship, created in Christ Jesus for good works, which God prepared beforehand that we should walk in them.

—EPHESIANS 2:4–10

Blessed be the God and Father of our Lord Jesus Christ, who has blessed us with every spiritual blessing in the heavenly places in Christ, just as He chose us in Him before the foundation of the world, that we should be holy and without blame before Him in love, having predestined us to adoption as sons by Jesus Christ to Himself, according to the good pleasure of His will, to the praise of the glory of His grace, by which He made us accepted in the Beloved. In Him we have redemption through His blood, the forgiveness of sins, according to the riches of His grace.

—EPHESIANS 1:3–7

The LORD has been mindful of us;
   He will bless us;
   He will bless the house of Israel;
   He will bless the house of Aaron.
He will bless those who fear the LORD,
   Both small and great.

—PSALM 115:12–13

But let all those rejoice who put their trust
      in You;
   Let them ever shout for joy, because You
      defend them;
   Let those also who love Your name
   Be joyful in You.
For You, O LORD, will bless the righteous;
   With favor You will surround him as with
      a shield.

—PSALM 5:11–12

Blessings are on the head of the righteous,
   But violence covers the mouth of the wicked.

The blessing of the LORD makes one rich,
   And He adds no sorrow with it.
To do evil is like sport to a fool,
   But a man of understanding has wisdom.
The fear of the wicked will come upon him,
   And the desire of the righteous will be granted.

—PROVERBS 10:6, 22–24

What the Bible Says About
SATAN

Beloved, do not believe every spirit, but test the spirits, whether they are of God; because many false prophets have gone out into the world. By this you know the Spirit of God: Every spirit that confesses that Jesus Christ has come in the flesh is of God, and every spirit that does not confess that Jesus Christ has come in the flesh is not of God. And this is the *spirit* of the Antichrist, which you have heard was coming, and is now already in the world. You are of God, little children, and have overcome them, because He who is in you is greater than he who is in the world.

—1 JOHN 4:1–4

Therefore submit to God. Resist the devil and he will flee from you. Draw near to God and He will draw near to you. Cleanse your hands, you sinners; and purify your hearts, you double-minded.

—JAMES 4:7–8

Finally, my brethren, be strong in the Lord and in the power of His might. Put on the whole armor of God, that you may be able to stand against the wiles of the devil. For we do not wrestle against flesh and blood, but against principalities, against powers, against the rulers of the darkness of this age, against spiritual hosts of wickedness in the heavenly places. Therefore take up the whole armor of God, that you may be able to withstand in the evil day, and having done all, to stand. Stand therefore, having girded your waist with truth, having put on the breastplate of righteousness, and having shod your feet with the preparation of the gospel of peace; above all, taking the shield of faith with which you will be able to quench all the fiery darts of the wicked one. And take the helmet of salvation, and the sword of the Spirit, which is the word of God; praying always with all prayer and supplication in the Spirit, being watchful to this end with all perseverance and supplication for all the saints.

—Ephesians 6:10–18

Be sober, be vigilant; because your adversary the devil walks about like a roaring lion, seeking whom he may devour. Resist him, steadfast in the faith, knowing that the same sufferings are experienced by your brotherhood in the world.

—1 PETER 5:8–9

And you He made alive, who were dead in trespasses and sins, in which you once walked according to the course of this world, according to the prince of the power of the air, the spirit who now works in the sons of disobedience, among whom also we all once conducted ourselves in the lusts of our flesh, fulfilling the desires of the flesh and of the mind, and were by nature children of wrath, just as the others. But God, who is rich in mercy, because of His great love with which He loved us, even when we were dead in trespasses, made us alive together with Christ (by grace you have been saved), and raised us up together, and made us sit together in the heavenly places in Christ Jesus.

—EPHESIANS 2:1–6

The name of the LORD is a strong tower;
  The righteous run to it and are safe.

—PROVERBS 18:10

For though we walk in the flesh, we do not war according to the flesh. For the weapons of our warfare are not carnal but mighty in God for pulling down strongholds, casting down arguments and every high thing that exalts itself against the knowledge of God, bringing every thought into captivity to the obedience of Christ.

—2 CORINTHIANS 10:3–5

What the Bible Says About
THE RETURN OF CHRIST

But I do not want you to be ignorant, brethren, concerning those who have fallen asleep, lest you sorrow as others who have no hope. For if we believe that Jesus died and rose again, even so God will bring with Him those who sleep in Jesus. For this we say to you by the word of the Lord, that we who are alive and remain until the coming of the Lord will by no means precede those who are asleep. For the Lord Himself will descend from heaven with a shout, with the voice of an archangel, and with the trumpet of God. And the dead in Christ will rise first. Then we who are alive and remain shall be caught up together with them in the clouds to meet the Lord in the air. And thus we shall always be with the Lord. There-fore comfort one another with these words.

—1 THESSALONIANS 4:13–18

Behold, I tell you a mystery: We shall not all sleep, but we shall all be changed—in a moment, in the twinkling of an eye, at the last trumpet. For the trumpet will sound, and the dead will be raised incorruptible, and we shall be changed. For this corruptible must put on incorruption, and this mortal must put on immortality. So when this corruptible has put on incorruption, and this mortal has put on immortality, then shall be brought to pass the saying that is written: "*Death is swallowed up in victory.*"

"*O Death, where is your sting?*
O Hades, where is your victory?"
The sting of death is sin, and the strength of sin is the law. But thanks be to God, who gives us the victory through our Lord Jesus Christ.

—1 CORINTHIANS 15:51–57

Knowing this first: that scoffers will come in the last days, walking according to their own lusts, and saying, "Where is the promise of His coming? For since the fathers fell asleep, all things continue as they were from the beginning of creation."

But, beloved, do not forget this one thing, that with the Lord one day is as a thousand years, and a thousand years as one day. The Lord is not slack concerning His promise, as some count slackness, but is longsuffering toward us, not willing that any should perish but that all should come to repentance.

But the day of the Lord will come as a thief in the night, in which the heavens will pass away with a great noise, and the elements will melt with fervent heat; both the earth and the works that are in it will be burned up.

Therefore, since all these things will be dissolved, what manner of persons ought you to be in holy conduct and godliness, looking for and hastening the coming of the day of God, because of which the heavens will be dissolved, being on fire, and the elements will melt with fervent heat? Nevertheless we, according to His promise, look for new heavens and a new earth in which righteousness dwells.

—2 PETER 3:3–4, 8–13

Beloved, now we are children of God; and it has not yet been revealed what we shall be, but we know that when He is revealed, we shall be like Him, for we shall see Him as He is. And everyone who has this hope in Him purifies himself, just as He is pure.

—1 JOHN 3:2–3

"For as the lightning comes from the east and flashes to the west, so also will the coming of the Son of Man be. . . .

"Immediately after the tribulation of those days the sun will be darkened, and the moon will not give its light; the stars will fall from heaven, and the powers of the heavens will be shaken.

"Then the sign of the Son of Man will appear in heaven, and then all the tribes of the earth will mourn, and they will see the Son of Man coming on the clouds of heaven with power and great glory. And He will send His angels with a great sound of a trumpet, and they will gather together His elect from the four winds, from one end of heaven to the other."

—MATTHEW 24:27, 29–31

"But of that day and hour no one knows, not even the angels of heaven, but My Father only. But as the days of Noah were, so also will the coming of the Son of Man be. For as in the days before the flood, they were eating and drinking, marrying and giving in marriage, until the day that Noah entered the ark, and did not know until the flood came and took them all away, so also will the coming of the Son of Man be. Then two men will be in the field: one will be taken and the other left. Two women will be grinding at the mill: one will be taken and the other left.

"Watch therefore, for you do not know what hour your Lord is coming. But know this, that if the master of the house had known what hour the thief would come, he would have watched and not allowed his house to be broken into. Therefore you also be ready, for the Son of Man is coming at an hour you do not expect."

—MATTHEW 24:36–44

Now as He sat on the Mount of Olives, the disciples came to Him privately, saying, "Tell us, when will these things be? And what will be the sign of Your coming, and of the end of the age?"

And Jesus answered and said to them: "Take heed that no one deceives you. For many will come in My name, saying, 'I am the Christ,' and will deceive many. And you will hear of wars and rumors of wars. See that you are not troubled; for all these things must come to pass, but the end is not yet. For nation will rise against nation, and kingdom against kingdom. And there will be famines, pestilences, and earthquakes in various places. All these are the beginning of sorrows.

"Then they will deliver you up to tribulation and kill you, and you will be hated by all nations for My name's sake. And then many will be offended, will betray one another, and will hate one another. Then many false prophets will rise up and deceive many. And because lawlessness will abound, the love of many will grow cold. But he who endures to the end shall be saved. And this gospel of the kingdom will be preached in all the world as a witness to all the nations, and then the end will come."

—MATTHEW 24:3–14

"And there will be signs in the sun, in the moon, and in the stars; and on the earth distress of nations, with perplexity, the sea and the waves roaring; men's hearts failing them from fear and the expectation of those things which are coming on the earth, for the powers of the heavens will be shaken. Then they will see the Son of Man coming in a cloud with power and great glory. Now when these things begin to happen, look up and lift up your heads, because your redemption draws near."

—LUKE 21:25–28

I charge you therefore before God and the Lord Jesus Christ, who will judge the living and the dead at His appearing and His kingdom: Preach the word! Be ready in season and out of season. Convince, rebuke, exhort, with all longsuffering and teaching. For the time will come when they will not endure sound doctrine, but according to their own desires, because they have itching ears, they will heap up for themselves teachers; and they will turn their ears away from the truth, and be turned aside to fables. But you be watchful in all things, endure afflictions, do the work of an evangelist, fulfill your ministry.

For I am already being poured out as a drink offering, and the time of my departure is at hand. I have fought the good fight, I have finished the race, I have kept the faith. Finally, there is laid up for me the crown of righteousness, which the Lord, the righteous Judge, will give to me on that Day, and not to me only but also to all who have loved His appearing.

—2 TIMOTHY 4:1–8

What the Bible Says About
GOD'S LOVE

In this is love, not that we loved God, but that He loved us and sent His Son to be the propitiation for our sins. Beloved, if God so loved us, we also ought to love one another. No one has seen God at any time. If we love one another, God abides in us, and His love has been perfected in us.

—1 JOHN 4:10–12

"As the Father loved Me, I also have loved you; abide in My love. If you keep My commandments, you will abide in My love, just as I have kept My Father's commandments and abide in His love."

—JOHN 15:9–10

But God demonstrates His own love toward us, in that while we were still sinners, Christ died for us.

—ROMANS 5:8

Beloved, let us love one another, for love is of God; and everyone who loves is born of God and knows God. He who does not love does not know God, for God is love.

—1 JOHN 4:7–8

The LORD has appeared of old to me, saying:
"Yes, I have loved you with an everlasting love;
Therefore with lovingkindness I have
drawn you."

—JEREMIAH 31:3

"For God so loved the world that He gave His only begotten Son, that whoever believes in Him should not perish but have everlasting life."

—JOHN 3:16

For I am persuaded that neither death nor life, nor angels nor principalities nor powers, nor things present nor things to come, nor height nor depth, nor any other created thing, shall be able to separate us from the love of God which is in Christ Jesus our Lord.

—ROMANS 8:38–39

When I consider Your heavens, the work of
    Your fingers,
  The moon and the stars, which You have
    ordained,
What is man that You are mindful of him,
  And the son of man that You visit with him?
For you have made him a little lower than the
    angels,
  And You have crowned him with glory and
    honor.

You have made him to have dominion over the
    works of Your hands;
  You have put all things under his feet,
All sheep and oxen—
  Even the beasts of the field,
The birds of the air,
  And the fish of the sea
  That pass through the paths of the seas.

O Lord, our Lord,
  How excellent is Your name in all the earth!
                                    —Psalm 8

O Lord, You have searched me and known me.
You know my sitting down and my rising up;
    You understand my thoughts afar off.
You comprehend my path and my lying down,
    And are acquainted with all my ways.
For there is not a word on my tongue,
    But behold, O Lord, you know it altogether.
You have hedged me behind and before,
    And laid Your hand upon me.
Such knowledge is too wonderful for me;
It is high, I cannot attain it.

—Psalm 139:1–6

"He who has My commandments and keeps
them, it is he who loves Me. And he who loves
Me will be loved by My Father, and I will love
him and manifest Myself to him."

—John 14:21

How to Let God Guide You in Your Relationships . . .

Hear, my son, and receive my sayings,
 And the years of your life will be many.
I have taught you in the way of wisdom;
 I have led you in right paths.
When you walk, your steps will not be
   hindered,
 And when you run, you will not stumble.
Take firm hold of instruction, do not
   let go;
 Keep her, for she is your life.

          —PROVERBS 4:10–13

How to Let God Guide You
in Your Relationships
WITH YOUR SPOUSE

Live joyfully with the wife whom you love
all the days of your vain life which He has
given you under the sun, all your days of
vanity; for that is your portion in life, and in
the labor which you perform under the sun.

—ECCLESIASTES 9:9

He who finds a wife finds a good thing,
　And obtains favor from the LORD.

—PROVERBS 18:22

Let your fountain be blessed,
　And rejoice with the wife of your youth.
As a loving deer and a graceful doe,
　Let her breasts satisfy you at all times;
And always be enraptured with her love.

—PROVERBS 5:18–19

And He answered and said to them, "Have
you not read that He who made them at the

beginning '*made them male and female,*' and said, '*For this reason a man shall leave his father and mother and be joined to his wife, and the two shall become one flesh*'? So then, they are no longer two but one flesh. Therefore what God has joined together, let not man separate."

—MATTHEW 19:4–6

How fair is your love,
    My sister, my spouse!
    How much better than wine is your love,
    And the scent of your perfumes
    Than all spices!
Your lips, O my spouse,
    Drip as the honeycomb;
    Honey and milk are under your tongue;
    And the fragrance of your garments
    Is like the fragrance of Lebanon.

A garden enclosed
    Is my sister, my spouse,
    A spring shut up,
    A fountain sealed.
Your plants are an orchard of pomegranates
    With pleasant fruits,
    Fragrant henna with spikenard,

Spikenard and saffron,
   Calamus and cinnamon,
   With all trees of frankincense,
   Myrrh and aloes,
   With all the chief spices—
A fountain of gardens,
   A well of living waters,
And streams from Lebanon.

Awake, O north wind,
   And come, O south!
   Blow upon my garden,
   That its spices may flow out.
   Let my beloved come to his garden
   And eat its pleasant fruits.

—SONG OF SOLOMON 4:10–16

Nevertheless, because of sexual immorality, let each man have his own wife, and let each woman have her own husband. Let the husband render to his wife the affection due her, and likewise also the wife to her husband. The wife does not have authority over her own body, but the husband does. And likewise the husband does not have authority over his own body, but the wife does. Do not deprive one another except with consent for a time, that you may give yourselves to fasting and prayer; and come together again so that Satan does not tempt you because of your lack of self-control. But I say this as a concession, not as a commandment.

—1 CORINTHIANS 7:2–6

Wives, submit to your own husbands, as to the Lord. For the husband is head of the wife, as also Christ is head of the church; and He is the Savior of the body. Therefore, just as the church is subject to Christ, so let the wives be to their own husbands in everything.

Husbands, love your wives, just as Christ also loved the church and gave Himself for her, that He might sanctify and cleanse her with the washing of water by the word, that He might present her to Himself a glorious church, not having spot or wrinkle or any such thing, but that she should be holy and without blemish. So husbands ought to love their own wives as their own bodies; he who loves his wife loves himself.

—EPHESIANS 5:22–28

Husbands, likewise, dwell with them with understanding, giving honor to the wife, as to the weaker vessel, and as being heirs together of the grace of life, that your prayers may not be hindered.

Finally, all of you be of one mind, having compassion for one another; love as brothers, be tenderhearted, be courteous; not returning evil for evil or reviling for reviling, but on the contrary blessing, knowing that you were called to this, that you may inherit a blessing. For

> "He who would love life
>   And see good days,
> Let him refrain his tongue from evil,
>   And his lips from speaking deceit.
> Let him turn away from evil and do good;
>   Let him seek peace and pursue it."

—1 PETER 3:7–11

How to Let God Guide You in Your Relationships
WITH YOUR CHILDREN

I write to you, little children,
> Because your sins are forgiven you for His
> name's sake.

I write to you, fathers,
> Because you have known Him who is from
> the beginning.

I write to you, young men,
> Because you have overcome the wicked one.

I write to you, little children,
> Because you have known the Father.

I have written to you, fathers,
> Because you have known Him who is from
> the beginning.

I have written to you, young men,
> Because you are strong, and the word of
> God abides in you,
> And you have overcome the wicked one.

Do not love the world or the things in the world. If anyone loves the world, the love of the Father is not in him. For all that is in the world—the lust of the flesh, the lust of the eyes, and the pride of life—is not of the Father but is of the world. And the world is passing away, and the lust of it; but he who does the will of God abides forever.

—1 John 2:12–17

Then He said: "A certain man had two sons. And the younger of them said to his father, 'Father, give me the portion of goods that falls to me.' So he divided to them his livelihood.

"And not many days after, the younger son gathered all together, journeyed to a far country, and there wasted his possessions with prodigal living. But when he had spent all, there arose a severe famine in that land, and he began to be in want. Then he went and joined himself to a citizen of that country, and he sent him into his fields to feed swine. And he would gladly have filled his stomach with the pods that the swine ate, and no one gave him anything.

"But when he came to himself, he said, 'How many of my father's hired servants have bread enough and to spare, and I perish with hunger! I will arise and go to my father, and will say to him, "Father, I have sinned against heaven and before you, and I am no longer worthy to be called your son. Make me like one of your hired servants."' And he arose and came to his father.

"But when he was still a great way off, his father saw him and had compassion, and ran and fell on his neck and kissed him.

"And the son said to him, 'Father, I have sinned against heaven and in your sight, and am no longer worthy to be called your son.'

"But the father said to his servants, 'Bring out the best robe and put it on him, and put a ring on his hand and sandals on his feet. And bring the fatted calf here and kill it, and let us eat and be merry; for this my son was dead and is alive again; he was lost and is found.' And they began to be merry."

—LUKE 15:11–24

Then Jesus called a little child to Him, set him in the midst of them, and said, "Assuredly, I say to you, unless you are converted and become as little children, you will by no means enter the kingdom of heaven. Therefore whoever humbles himself as this little child is the greatest in the kingdom of heaven.

"Whoever receives one little child like this in My name receives Me. But whoever causes one of these little ones who believe in Me to sin, it would be better for him if a millstone were hung around his neck, and he were drowned in the depth of the sea. . . .

"Take heed that you do not despise one of these little ones, for I say to you that in heaven their angels always see the face of My Father who is in heaven. For the Son of Man has come to save that which was lost.

"What do you think? If a man has a hundred sheep, and one of them goes astray, does he not leave the ninety-nine and go to the mountains to seek the one that is straying? And if he should find it, assuredly, I say to you, he rejoices more over that sheep than over the ninety-nine that did not go astray. Even so it is not the will of your Father who is in heaven that one of these little ones should perish."

—MATTHEW 18:2–6, 10–14

"And these words which I command you today shall be in your heart. You shall teach them diligently to your children, and shall talk of them when you sit in your house, when you walk by the way, when you lie down, and when you rise up. You shall bind them as a sign on your hand, and they shall be as frontlets between your eyes. You shall write them on the doorposts of your house and on your gates."

—DEUTERONOMY 6:6–9

Behold, children are a heritage from the LORD,
    The fruit of the womb is a reward.
Like arrows in the hand of a warrior,
    So are the children of one's youth.
Happy is the man who has his quiver full of them;
    They shall not be ashamed,
        But shall speak with their enemies in the gate.

—PSALM 127:3–5

The righteous man walks in his integrity;
    His children are blessed after him.

—PROVERBS 20:7

Therefore be imitators of God as dear children. And walk in love, as Christ also has loved us and given Himself for us, an offering and a sacrifice to God for a sweet-smelling aroma.

—EPHESIANS 5:1–2

How to Let God Guide You in Your Relationships
WITH YOUR FRIENDS

That which we have seen and heard we declare to you, that you also may have fellowship with us; and truly our fellowship is with the Father and with His Son Jesus Christ.

But if we walk in the light as He is in the light, we have fellowship with one another, and the blood of Jesus Christ His Son cleanses us from all sin.

—1 JOHN 1:3, 7

But he, wanting to justify himself, said to Jesus, "And who is my neighbor?"

Then Jesus answered and said: "A certain man went down from Jerusalem to Jericho, and fell among thieves, who stripped him of his clothing, wounded him, and departed, leaving him half dead. Now by chance a certain priest came down that road. And when he saw him, he passed by on the other side. Likewise a Levite, when he arrived at the place, came and looked, and passed by on the other side. But a certain Samaritan, as he journeyed, came where he was. And when he saw him, he had compassion. So he went to him and bandaged his wounds, pouring on oil and wine; and he set him on his own animal, brought him to an inn, and took care of him. On the next day, when he departed, he took out two denarii, gave them to the innkeeper, and said to him, 'Take care of him; and whatever more you spend, when I come again, I will repay you.'

"So which of these three do you think was neighbor to him who fell among the thieves?"

And he said, "He who showed mercy on him." Then Jesus said to him, "Go and do likewise."

—LUKE 10:29–37

Do not forsake your own friend or your
    father's friend,
  Nor go to your brother's house in the day
    of your calamity;
  Better is a neighbor nearby than a brother
    far away.

—PROVERBS 27:10

Do not withhold good from those to whom it
    is due,
    When it is in the power of your hand to
        do so.
Do not say to your neighbor,
    "Go, and come back,
    And tomorrow I will give it,"
    When you have it with you.
Do not devise evil against your neighbor,
    For he dwells by you for safety's sake.
Do not strive with a man without cause,
    If he has done you no harm.

—PROVERBS 3:27–30

A man who has friends must himself be friendly,
    But there is a friend who sticks closer than
        a brother.

—PROVERBS 18:24

A friend loves at all times,
    And a brother is born for adversity.

—PROVERBS 17:17

"Greater love has no one than this, than to lay down one's life for his friends. You are My friends if you do whatever I command you. No longer do I call you servants, for a servant does not know what his master is doing; but I have called you friends, for all things that I heard from My Father I have made known to you."

—JOHN 15:13–15

How to Let God Guide You
in Your Relationships
WITH OTHER CHRISTIANS

Now, therefore, you are no longer strangers and foreigners, but fellow citizens with the saints and members of the household of God, having been built on the foundation of the apostles and prophets, Jesus Christ Himself being the chief cornerstone, in whom the whole building, being fitted together, grows into a holy temple in the Lord, in whom you also are being built together for a dwelling place of God in the Spirit.

—EPHESIANS 2:19–22

Finally, all of you be of one mind, having compassion for one another; love as brothers, be tenderhearted, be courteous; not returning evil for evil or reviling for reviling, but on the contrary blessing, knowing that you were called to this, that you may inherit a blessing.

—1 PETER 3:8–9

But now God has set the members, each one of them, in the body just as He pleased. And if they were all one member, where would the body be? But now indeed there are many members, yet one body.

And the eye cannot say to the hand, "I have no need of you"; nor again the head to the feet, "I have no need of you." No, much rather, those members of the body which seem to be weaker are necessary. And those members of the body which we think to be less honorable, on these we bestow greater honor; and our unpresentable parts have greater modesty, but our presentable parts have no need. But God composed the body, having given greater honor to that part which lacks it, that there should be no schism in the body, but that the members should have the same care for one another. And if one member suffers, all the members suffer with it; or if one member is honored, all the members rejoice with it.

Now you are the body of Christ, and members individually.

—1 Corinthians 12:18–27

"You call Me Teacher and Lord, and you say well, for so I am. If I then, your Lord and Teacher, have washed your feet, you also ought to wash one another's feet. For I have given you an example, that you should do as I have done to you. Most assuredly, I say to you, a servant is not greater than his master; nor is he who is sent greater than he who sent him. If you know these things, blessed are you if you do them."

—JOHN 13:13–17

"I do not pray for these alone, but also for those who will believe in Me through their word; that they all may be one, as You, Father, are in Me, and I in You; that they also may be one in Us, that the world may believe that You sent Me. And the glory which You gave Me I have given them, that they may be one just as We are one: I in them, and You in Me; that they may be made perfect in one, and that the world may know that You have sent Me, and have loved them as You have loved Me."

—JOHN 17:20–23

Be kindly affectionate to one another with brotherly love, in honor giving preference to one another.

—ROMANS 12:10

I, therefore, the prisoner of the Lord, beseech you to walk worthy of the calling with which you were called, with all lowliness and gentleness, with longsuffering, bearing with one another in love, endeavoring to keep the unity of the Spirit in the bond of peace.

—EPHESIANS 4:1–3

How to Let God Guide You
in Your Relationships
WITH YOUR FINANCES

"Now it shall come to pass, if you diligently obey the voice of the LORD your God, to observe carefully all His commandments which I command you today, that the LORD your God will set you high above all nations of the earth. And all these blessings shall come upon you and overtake you, because you obey the voice of the LORD your God:

"Blessed shall you be in the city, and blessed shall you be in the country.

"Blessed shall be the fruit of your body, the produce of your ground and the increase of your herds, the increase of your cattle and the offspring of your flocks.

"Blessed shall be your basket and your kneading bowl.

"Blessed shall you be when you come in, and blessed shall you be when you go out.

—DEUTERONOMY 28:1–6

Trust in the LORD, and do good;
    Dwell in the land, and feed on His faithfulness.
Delight yourself also in the LORD,
    And He shall give you the desires of your
        heart.

Commit your way to the LORD,
    Trust also in Him,
    And He shall bring it to pass.

—PSALM 37:3–5

"The LORD makes poor and makes rich;
    He brings low and lifts up.
He raises the poor from the dust
    And lifts the beggar from the ash heap,
    To set them among princes
    And make them inherit the throne of glory.

"For the pillars of the earth are the LORD's,
    And He has set the world upon them.
He will guard the feet of His saints,
    But the wicked shall be silent in darkness.

"For by strength no man shall prevail."

—1 SAMUEL 2:7–9

"Bring all the tithes into the storehouse,
  That there may be food in My house,
  And try Me now in this,"
  Says the LORD of hosts,
  "If I will not open for you the windows of
      heaven
  And pour out for you such blessing
  That there will not be room enough to
      receive it."

—MALACHI 3:10

Jesus said to him, "If you want to be perfect, go, sell what you have and give to the poor, and you will have treasure in heaven; and come, follow Me."

But when the young man heard that saying, he went away sorrowful, for he had great possessions.

Then Jesus said to His disciples, "Assuredly, I say to you that it is hard for a rich man to enter the kingdom of heaven. And again I say to you, it is easier for a camel to go through the eye of a needle than for a rich man to enter the kingdom of God."

—MATTHEW 19:21–24

What does it profit, my brethren, if someone says he has faith but does not have works? Can faith save him? If a brother or sister is naked and destitute of daily food, and one of you says to them, "Depart in peace, be warmed and filled," but you do not give them the things which are needed for the body, what does it profit? Thus also faith by itself, if it does not have works, is dead.

—JAMES 2:14–17

"Do not lay up for yourselves treasures on earth, where moth and rust destroy and where thieves break in and steal; but lay up for yourselves treasures in heaven, where neither moth nor rust destroys and where thieves do not break in and steal. For where your treasure is, there your heart will be also."

—MATTHEW 6:19–21

How to Let God Guide You in Your Relationships
WITH YOUR CHURCH

This is the message which we have heard from Him and declare to you, that God is light and in Him is no darkness at all. If we say that we have fellowship with Him, and walk in darkness, we lie and do not practice the truth. But if we walk in the light as He is in the light, we have fellowship with one another, and the blood of Jesus Christ His Son cleanses us from all sin.

—1 JOHN 1:5–7

God is faithful, by whom you were called into the fellowship of His Son, Jesus Christ our Lord.

Now I plead with you, brethren, by the name of our Lord Jesus Christ, that you all speak the same thing, and that there be no divisions among you, but that you be perfectly joined together in the same mind and in the same judgment.

—1 CORINTHIANS 1:9–10

For we are God's fellow workers; you are God's field, you are God's building.

According to the grace of God which was given to me, as a wise master builder I have laid the foundation, and another builds on it. But let each one take heed how he builds on it. For no other foundation can anyone lay than that which is laid, which is Jesus Christ. Now if anyone builds on this foundation with gold, silver, precious stones, wood, hay, straw, each one's work will become clear; for the Day will declare it, because it will be revealed by fire; and the fire will test each one's work, of what sort it is. If anyone's work which he has built on it endures, he will receive a reward.

—1 Corinthians 3:9–14

"For where two or three are gathered together in My name, I am there in the midst of them."

—Matthew 18:20

For whatever things were written before were written for our learning, that we through the patience and comfort of the Scriptures might have hope. Now may the God of patience and comfort grant you to be like-minded toward one another, according to Christ Jesus, that you may with one mind and one mouth glorify the God and Father of our Lord Jesus Christ.

Therefore receive one another, just as Christ also received us, to the glory of God.

—ROMANS 15:4–7

How to Let God Guide You
in Your Relationships
WITH YOUR ENEMIES

"But I say to you who hear: Love your enemies, do good to those who hate you, bless those who curse you, and pray for those who spitefully use you. To him who strikes you on the one cheek, offer the other also. And from him who takes away your cloak, do not withhold your tunic either. Give to everyone who asks of you. And from him who takes away your goods do not ask them back. And just as you want men to do to you, you also do to them likewise.

—LUKE 6:27–31

Give ear, O LORD, to my prayer;
    And attend to the voice of my supplications.
In the day of my trouble I will call upon You,
    For You will answer me.

—PSALM 86:6–7

Repay no one evil for evil. Have regard for good things in the sight of all men. If it is possible, as much as depends on you, live peaceably with all men. Beloved, do not avenge yourselves, but rather give place to wrath; for it is written, *"Vengeance is Mine, I will repay,"* says the Lord. Therefore

> *"If your enemy is hungry, feed him;*
> *If he is thirsty, give him a drink;*
> *For in so doing you will heap coals of fire on his head."*

Do not be overcome by evil, but overcome evil with good.

—ROMANS 12:17–21

If your enemy is hungry, give him bread to eat;
And if he is thirsty, give him water to drink;
For so you will heap coals of fire on his head,
And the LORD will reward you.

—PROVERBS 25:21–22

Do not rejoice when your enemy falls,
  And do not let your heart be glad when
    he stumbles;
Lest the LORD see it, and it displease Him,
  And He turn away His wrath from him.

Do not fret because of evildoers,
  Nor be envious of the wicked;
For there will be no prospect for the evil man;
  The lamp of the wicked will be put out.

—PROVERBS 24:17–20

But the Lord is faithful, who will establish
you and guard you from the evil one.

—2 THESSALONIANS 3:3

For the LORD your God is He who goes with
you, to fight for you against your enemies, to
save you.

—DEUTERONOMY 20:4

"You have heard that it was said, '*You shall love your neighbor* and hate your enemy.' But I say to you, love your enemies, bless those who curse you, do good to those who hate you, and pray for those who spitefully use you and persecute you, that you may be sons of your Father in heaven; for He makes His sun rise on the evil and on the good, and sends rain on the just and on the unjust."

—MATTHEW 5:43–45

Discovering God Is . . .

That the God of our Lord Jesus Christ, the Father of glory, may give to you the spirit of wisdom and revelation in the knowledge of Him, the eyes of your understanding being enlightened; that you may know what is the hope of His calling, what are the riches of the glory of His inheritance in the saints, and what is the exceeding greatness of His power toward us who believe, according to the working of His mighty power.

—EPHESIANS 1:17–19

Discovering God Is
GOD'S PLAN OF SALVATION

For all have sinned and fall short of the glory of God, being justified freely by His grace through the redemption that is in Christ Jesus, whom God set forth as a propitiation by His blood, through faith, to demonstrate His righteousness, because in His forbearance God had passed over the sins that were previously committed, to demonstrate at the present time His righteousness, that He might be just and the justifier of the one who has faith in Jesus.

—ROMANS 3:23–26

"For God so loved the world that He gave His only begotten Son, that whoever believes in Him should not perish but have everlasting life. For God did not send His Son into the world to condemn the world, but that the world through Him might be saved."

—JOHN 3:16–17

But God demonstrates His own love toward us, in that while we were still sinners, Christ died for us.

Much more then, having now been justified by His blood, we shall be saved from wrath through Him. For if when we were enemies we were reconciled to God through the death of His Son, much more, having been reconciled, we shall be saved by His life. And not only that, but we also rejoice in God through our Lord Jesus Christ, through whom we have now received the reconciliation.

—ROMANS 5:8–11

And this is the testimony: that God has given us eternal life, and this life is in His Son. He who has the Son has life; he who does not have the Son of God does not have life.

These things I have written to you who believe in the name of the Son of God, that you may know that you have eternal life, and that you may continue to believe in the name of the Son of God.

—1 JOHN 5:11–13

"He who believes in the Son has everlasting life; and he who does not believe the Son shall not see life, but the wrath of God abides on him."

—JOHN 3:36

For by grace you have been saved through faith, and that not of yourselves; it is the gift of God, not of works, lest anyone should boast. For we are His workmanship, created in Christ Jesus for good works, which God prepared beforehand that we should walk in them.

—EPHESIANS 2:8–10

That if you confess with your mouth the Lord Jesus and believe in your heart that God has raised Him from the dead, you will be saved. For with the heart one believes unto righteousness, and with the mouth confession is made unto salvation.

—ROMANS 10:9–10

For the wages of sin is death, but the gift of God is eternal life in Christ Jesus our Lord.

—ROMANS 6:23

"Behold, I stand at the door and knock. If anyone hears My voice and opens the door, I will come in to him and dine with him, and he with Me."

—Revelation 3:20

Discovering God Is
EXPERIENCING
GOD'S FORGIVENESS

Bless the LORD, O my soul,
  And forget not all His benefits:
Who forgives all your iniquities,
  Who heals all your diseases,
Who redeems your life from destruction,
  Who crowns you with lovingkindness and
    tender mercies.

—PSALM 103:2–4

For as the heavens are high above the earth,
  So great is His mercy toward those who
    fear Him;
As far as the east is from the west,
  So far has He removed our transgressions
    from us.

—PSALM 103:11–12

And you, being dead in your trespasses and
the uncircumcision of your flesh, He has made
alive together with Him, having forgiven you

all trespasses, having wiped out the hand-
writing of requirements that was against us,
which was contrary to us. And He has taken it
out of the way, having nailed it to the cross.

—COLOSSIANS 2:13–14

If You, LORD, should mark iniquities,
    O Lord, who could stand?
But there is forgiveness with You,
    That You may be feared.

—PSALM 130:3–4

"But this is the covenant that I will make
with the house of Israel after those days, says
the LORD: I will put My law in their minds, and
write it on their hearts; and I will be their God,
and they shall be My people. No more shall
every man teach his neighbor, and every man
his brother, saying, 'Know the LORD,' for they
all shall know Me, from the least of them to
the greatest of them, says the LORD. For I will
forgive their iniquity, and their sin I will
remember no more."

—JEREMIAH 31:33–34

If we say that we have no sin, we deceive ourselves, and the truth is not in us. If we confess our sins, He is faithful and just to forgive us our sins and to cleanse us from all unrighteousness.

—1 JOHN 1:8–9

In Him we have redemption through His blood, the forgiveness of sins, according to the riches of His grace which He made to abound toward us in all wisdom and prudence.

—EPHESIANS 1:7–8

Discovering God Is
UNDERSTANDING THE HOLY SPIRIT

⤶⤷

"And I will pray the Father, and He will give you another Helper, that He may abide with you forever—the Spirit of truth, whom the world cannot receive, because it neither sees Him nor knows Him; but you know Him, for He dwells with you and will be in you."

—JOHN 14:16–17

When the Day of Pentecost had fully come, they were all with one accord in one place. And suddenly there came a sound from heaven, as of a rushing mighty wind, and it filled the whole house where they were sitting. Then there appeared to them divided tongues, as of fire, and one sat upon each of them. And they were all filled with the Holy Spirit and began to speak with other tongues, as the Spirit gave them utterance.

—ACTS 2:1–4

"But when the Helper comes, whom I shall send to you from the Father, the Spirit of truth who proceeds from the Father, He will testify of Me."

—JOHN 15:26

Therefore they gathered them up, and filled twelve baskets with the fragments of the five barley loaves which were left over by those who had eaten.

Then those men, when they had seen the sign that Jesus did, said, "This is truly the Prophet who is to come into the world."

—JOHN 6:13–14

"And anyone who speaks a word against the Son of Man, it will be forgiven him; but to him who blasphemes against the Holy Spirit, it will not be forgiven.

"Now when they bring you to the synagogues and magistrates and authorities, do not worry about how or what you should answer, or what you should say. For the Holy Spirit will teach you in that very hour what you ought to say."

—LUKE 12:10–12

"But you shall receive power when the Holy Spirit has come upon you; and you shall be witnesses to Me in Jerusalem, and in all Judea and Samaria, and to the end of the earth."

—ACTS 1:8

But God has revealed them to us through His Spirit.

For the Spirit searches all things, yes, the deep things of God. For what man knows the things of a man except the spirit of the man which is in him? Even so no one knows the things of God except the Spirit of God. Now we have received, not the spirit of the world, but the Spirit who is from God, that we might know the things that have been freely given to us by God. These things we also speak, not in words which man's wisdom teaches but which the Holy Spirit teaches, comparing spiritual things with spiritual. But the natural man does not receive the things of the Spirit of God, for they are foolishness to him; nor can he know them, because they are spiritually discerned. But he who is spiritual judges all things, yet he himself is rightly judged by no one.

—1 CORINTHIANS 2:10–15

And if Christ is in you, the body is dead because of sin, but the Spirit is life because of righteousness. But if the Spirit of Him who raised Jesus from the dead dwells in you, He who raised Christ from the dead will also give life to your mortal bodies through His Spirit who dwells in you.

Therefore, brethren, we are debtors—not to the flesh, to live according to the flesh. For if you live according to the flesh you will die; but if by the Spirit you put to death the deeds of the body, you will live. For as many as are led by the Spirit of God, these are sons of God. For you did not receive the spirit of bondage again to fear, but you received the Spirit of adoption by whom we cry out, "Abba, Father." The Spirit Himself bears witness with our spirit that we are children of God, and if children, then heirs—heirs of God and joint heirs with Christ, if indeed we suffer with Him, that we may also be glorified together.

—ROMANS 8:10–17

Discovering God Is
WHAT JESUS IS TO YOU

For He Himself is our peace, who has made both one, and has broken down the middle wall of separation, having abolished in His flesh the enmity, that is, the law of commandments contained in ordinances, so as to create in Himself one new man from the two, thus making peace, and that He might reconcile them both to God in one body through the cross, thereby putting to death the enmity. And He came and preached peace to you who were afar off and to those who were near. For through Him we both have access by one Spirit to the Father.

Now, therefore, you are no longer strangers and foreigners, but fellow citizens with the saints and members of the household of God.

—EPHESIANS 2:14–19

And we have seen and testify that the Father has sent the Son as Savior of the world. Whoever confesses that Jesus is the Son of God, God abides in him, and he in God.

—1 JOHN 4:14–15

Let this mind be in you which was also in Christ Jesus, who, being in the form of God, did not consider it robbery to be equal with God, but made Himself of no reputation, taking the form of a bondservant, and coming in the likeness of men. And being found in appearance as a man, He humbled Himself and became obedient to the point of death, even the death of the cross. Therefore God also has highly exalted Him and given Him the name which is above every name, that at the name of Jesus every knee should bow, of those in heaven, and of those on earth, and of those under the earth, and that every tongue should confess that Jesus Christ is Lord, to the glory of God the Father.

—PHILIPPIANS 2:5–11

Jesus said to her, "I am the resurrection and the life. He who believes in Me, though he may die, he shall live. And whoever lives and believes in Me shall never die. Do you believe this?"

—JOHN 11:25–26

Therefore we also, since we are surrounded by so great a cloud of witnesses, let us lay aside every weight, and the sin which so easily ensnares us, and let us run with endurance the race that is set before us, looking unto Jesus, the author and finisher of our faith, who for the joy that was set before Him endured the cross, despising the shame, and has sat down at the right hand of the throne of God.

—HEBREWS 12:1–2

Then Jesus said to them again, "Most assuredly, I say to you, I am the door of the sheep. All who ever came before Me are thieves and robbers, but the sheep did not hear them. I am the door. If anyone enters by Me, he will be saved, and will go in and out and find pasture. The thief does not come except to steal, and to kill, and to destroy. I have come that they may have life, and that they may have it more abundantly.

"I am the good shepherd. The good shepherd gives His life for the sheep."

—JOHN 10:7–11

And Jesus said to them, "I am the bread of life. He who comes to Me shall never hunger, and he who believes in Me shall never thirst. But I said to you that you have seen Me and yet do not believe. All that the Father gives Me will come to Me, and the one who comes to Me I will by no means cast out. For I have come down from heaven, not to do My own will, but the will of Him who sent Me. This is the will of the Father who sent Me, that of all He has given Me I should lose nothing, but should raise it up at the last day. And this is the will of Him who sent Me, that everyone who sees the Son and believes in Him may have everlasting life; and I will raise him up at the last day."

—JOHN 6:35–40

Walking
with God Is . . .

Incline your ear and hear the words
of the wise,
And apply your heart to my knowledge;
For it is a pleasant thing if you keep them
within you;
Let them all be fixed upon your lips,
So that your trust may be in the LORD.

—PROVERBS 22:17–19A

Walking with God Is
TRUSTING GOD

Trust in the LORD with all your heart,
    And lean not on your own understanding;
In all your ways acknowledge Him,
    And He shall direct your paths.

—PROVERBS 3:5–6

But let all those rejoice who put their trust
       in You;
    Let them ever shout for joy, because You
       defend them;
    Let those also who love Your name
    Be joyful in You.
For You, O LORD, will bless the righteous;
    With favor You will surround him as with
       a shield.

—PSALM 5:11–12

The fear of man brings a snare,
    But whoever trusts in the LORD shall be safe.

—PROVERBS 29:25

The LORD also will be a refuge for the oppressed,
    A refuge in times of trouble.
And those who know Your name will put their
    trust in You;
    For You, LORD, have not forsaken those who
    seek You.

—PSALM 9:9–10

I have called upon You, for You will hear me,
    O God;
    Incline Your ear to me, and hear my speech.
Show Your marvelous lovingkindness by Your
    right hand,
    O You who save those who trust in You
    From those who rise up against them.
Keep me as the apple of Your eye;
    Hide me under the shadow of Your wings.

—PSALM 17:6–8

He who is of a proud heart stirs up strife,
    But he who trusts in the LORD will be
    prospered.
He who trusts in his own heart is a fool,
    But whoever walks wisely will be delivered.

—PROVERBS 28:25–26

The LORD is my rock and my fortress and my
      deliverer;
    My God, my strength, in whom I will trust;
    My shield and the horn of my salvation, my
      stronghold.
I will call upon the LORD, who is worthy to
      be praised;
    So shall I be saved from my enemies.

                   —PSALM 18:2–3

The LORD is near to those who have a broken
      heart,
    And saves such as have a contrite spirit.

Many are the afflictions of the righteous,
    But the LORD delivers him out of them all.
He guards all his bones;
    Not one of them is broken.
Evil shall slay the wicked,
    And those who hate the righteous shall
      be condemned.
The LORD redeems the soul of His servants,
    And none of those who trust in Him shall
      be condemned.

                   —PSALM 34:18–22

Trust in the LORD, and do good;
    Dwell in the land, and feed on His faithfulness.
Delight yourself also in the LORD,
    And He shall give you the desires of your
        heart.

Commit your way to the LORD,
    Trust also in Him,
    And He shall bring it to pass.

He shall bring forth your righteousness as
        the light,
    And your justice as the noonday.

                                    —PSALM 37:3–6

Walking with God Is
CONTINUAL PRAYER

Is anyone among you suffering? Let him pray. Is anyone cheerful? Let him sing psalms. Is anyone among you sick? Let him call for the elders of the church, and let them pray over him, anointing him with oil in the name of the Lord. And the prayer of faith will save the sick, and the Lord will raise him up. And if he has committed sins, he will be forgiven. Confess your trespasses to one another, and pray for one another, that you may be healed. The effective, fervent prayer of a righteous man avails much.

—JAMES 5:13–16

Now this is the confidence that we have in Him, that if we ask anything according to His will, He hears us. And if we know that He hears us, whatever we ask, we know that we have the petitions that we have asked of Him.

—1 JOHN 5:14–15

Rejoice in the Lord always. Again I will say, rejoice! Let your gentleness be known to all men. The Lord is at hand. Be anxious for nothing, but in everything by prayer and supplication, with thanksgiving, let your requests be made known to God; and the peace of God, which surpasses all understanding, will guard your hearts and minds through Christ Jesus.

—Philippians 4:4–7

"Our Father in heaven,
    Hallowed be Your name.
    Your kingdom come.
    Your will be done
    On earth as it is in heaven.
    Give us this day our daily bread.
    And forgive us our debts,
    As we forgive our debtors.
    And do not lead us into temptation,
    But deliver us from the evil one.
    For Yours is the kingdom and the power
    and the glory forever. Amen."

—Matthew 6:9b–13

Rejoice always, pray without ceasing, in everything give thanks; for this is the will of God in Christ Jesus for you.

—1 Thessalonians 5:16–18

So Jesus answered and said to them, "Have faith in God. For assuredly, I say to you, whoever says to this mountain, 'Be removed and be cast into the sea,' and does not doubt in his heart, but believes that those things he says will be done, he will have whatever he says. Therefore I say to you, whatever things you ask when you pray, believe that you receive them, and you will have them.

"And whenever you stand praying, if you have anything against anyone, forgive him, that your Father in heaven may also forgive you your trespasses."

—Mark 11:22–25

"Call to Me, and I will answer you, and show you great and mighty things, which you do not know."

—Jeremiah 33:3

"If My people who are called by My name will humble themselves, and pray and seek My face, and turn from their wicked ways, then I will hear from heaven, and will forgive their sin and heal their land."

—2 Chronicles 7:14

Walking with God Is
FINDING GOD'S WILL

You are my hiding place;
    You shall preserve me from trouble;
    You shall surround me with songs of
        deliverance.

I will instruct you and teach you in the way
            you should go;
    I will guide you with My eye.

Many sorrows shall be to the wicked;
    But he who trusts in the LORD, mercy shall
        surround him.

—PSALM 32:7–8, 10

Therefore submit yourselves to every
ordinance of man for the Lord's sake, whether
to the king as supreme, or to governors, as to
those who are sent by him for the punishment
of evildoers and for the praise of those who do
good. For this is the will of God, that by doing
good you may put to silence the ignorance of
foolish men.

—1 PETER 2:13–15

All the ways of a man are pure in his own eyes,
   But the LORD weighs the spirits.

Commit your works to the LORD,
   And your thoughts will be established.

—PROVERBS 16:2–3

Finally then, brethren, we urge and exhort in the Lord Jesus that you should abound more and more, just as you received from us how you ought to walk and to please God; for you know what commandments we gave you through the Lord Jesus.

For this is the will of God, your sanctification: that you should abstain from sexual immorality; that each of you should know how to possess his own vessel in sanctification and honor, not in passion of lust, like the Gentiles who do not know God; that no one should take advantage of and defraud his brother in this matter, because the Lord is the avenger of all such, as we also forewarned you and testified. For God did not call us to uncleanness, but in holiness.

—1 THESSALONIANS 4:1–7

See then that you walk circumspectly, not as fools but as wise, redeeming the time, because the days are evil. Therefore do not be unwise, but understand what the will of the Lord is.

—EPHESIANS 5:15–17

My son, keep your father's command,
And do not forsake the law of your mother.
Bind them continually upon your heart;
Tie them around your neck.
When you roam, they will lead you;
When you sleep, they will keep you;
And when you awake, they will speak with you.
For the commandment is a lamp,
And the law a light;
Reproofs of instruction are the way of life.

—PROVERBS 6:20–23

Search me, O God, and know my heart;
Try me, and know my anxieties;
And see if there is any wicked way in me,
And lead me in the way everlasting.

—PSALM 139:23–24

Walking with God Is
DEVELOPING A
DISCERNING SPIRIT

Let us therefore be diligent to enter that rest, lest anyone fall according to the same example of disobedience.

For the word of God is living and powerful, and sharper than any two-edged sword, piercing even to the division of soul and spirit, and of joints and marrow, and is a discerner of the thoughts and intents of the heart. And there is no creature hidden from His sight, but all things are naked and open to the eyes of Him to whom we must give account.

—HEBREWS 4:11–13

He who keeps his command will experience
    nothing harmful;
  And a wise man's heart discerns both time
    and judgment,
Because for every matter there is a time and
    judgment.

—ECCLESIASTES 8:5–6A

For this reason I bow my knees to the Father of our Lord Jesus Christ, from whom the whole family in heaven and earth is named, that He would grant you, according to the riches of His glory, to be strengthened with might through His Spirit in the inner man, that Christ may dwell in your hearts through faith; that you, being rooted and grounded in love, may be able to comprehend with all the saints what is the width and length and depth and height—to know the love of Christ which passes knowledge; that you may be filled with all the fullness of God.

—Ephesians 3:14–19

But the natural man does not receive the things of the Spirit of God, for they are foolishness to him; nor can he know them, because they are spiritually discerned. But he who is spiritual judges all things, yet he himself is rightly judged by no one. For "*who has known the mind of the Lord that he may instruct Him?*" But we have the mind of Christ.

—1 Corinthians 2:14–16

To know wisdom and instruction,
  To perceive the words of understanding,
To receive the instruction of wisdom,
  Justice, judgment, and equity;
To give prudence to the simple,
  To the young man knowledge and discretion—
A wise man will hear and increase learning,
  And a man of understanding will attain
    wise counsel.

—PROVERBS 1:2–5

Walking with God Is RECOGNIZING GOD'S CORRECTION

My son, do not despise the chastening of
    the LORD,
  Nor detest His correction;
For whom the LORD loves He corrects,
  Just as a father the son in whom he delights.

—PROVERBS 3:11–12

The LORD knows the thoughts of man,
  That they are futile.

Blessed is the man whom You instruct, O LORD,
  And teach out of Your law,
That You may give him rest from the days
    of adversity,
  Until the pit is dug for the wicked.
For the LORD will not cast off His people,
  Nor will He forsake His inheritance.
But judgment will return to righteousness,
  And all the upright in heart will follow it.

—PSALM 94:11–15

If you endure chastening, God deals with you as with sons; for what son is there whom a father does not chasten? But if you are without chastening, of which all have become partakers, then you are illegitimate and not sons. Furthermore, we have had human fathers who corrected us, and we paid them respect. Shall we not much more readily be in subjection to the Father of spirits and live? For they indeed for a few days chastened us as seemed best to them, but He for our profit, that we may be partakers of His holiness. Now no chastening seems to be joyful for the present, but painful; nevertheless, afterward it yields the peaceable fruit of righteousness to those who have been trained by it.

—HEBREWS 12:7–11

All Scripture is given by inspiration of God, and is profitable for doctrine, for reproof, for correction, for instruction in righteousness, that the man of God may be complete, thoroughly equipped for every good work.

—2 TIMOTHY 3:16–17

"Behold, I set before you today a blessing and a curse: the blessing, if you obey the commandments of the LORD your God which I command you today; and the curse, if you do not obey the commandments of the LORD your God, but turn aside from the way which I command you today, to go after other gods which you have not known.

—DEUTERONOMY 11:26–28

The labor of the righteous leads to life,
    The wages of the wicked to sin.

He who keeps instruction is in the way of life,
    But he who refuses correction goes astray.

—PROVERBS 10:16–17

Walking with God Is
KNOWING
YOUR BEST FRIEND

Let all those who seek You rejoice and be glad
    in You;
    Let such as love Your salvation say continually,
    "The LORD be magnified!"
But I am poor and needy;
    Yet the LORD thinks upon me.
    You are my help and my deliverer;
    Do not delay, O my God.

—PSALM 40:16–17

A man who has friends must himself be friendly,
    But there is a friend who sticks closer than
        a brother.

—PROVERBS 18:24

Our soul waits for the LORD;
    He is our help and our shield.
For our heart shall rejoice in Him,
    Because we have trusted in His holy name.
Let Your mercy, O LORD, be upon us,
    Just as we hope in You.

—PSALM 33:20–22

"Greater love has no one than this, than to lay down one's life for his friends. You are My friends if you do whatever I command you. No longer do I call you servants, for a servant does not know what his master is doing; but I have called you friends, for all things that I heard from My Father I have made known to you. You did not choose Me, but I chose you and appointed you that you should go and bear fruit, and that your fruit should remain, that whatever you ask the Father in My name He may give you. These things I command you, that you love one another."

—JOHN 15:13–17

But the salvation of the righteous is from
    the LORD;
  He is their strength in the time of trouble.
And the LORD shall help them and deliver
    them;
  He shall deliver them from the wicked,
  And save them,
  Because they trust in Him.

—PSALM 37:39–40

I will lift up my eyes to the hills—
From whence comes my help?
My help comes from the LORD,
Who made heaven and earth.

He will not allow your foot to be moved;
He who keeps you will not slumber.
Behold, He who keeps Israel
Shall neither slumber nor sleep.

The LORD is your keeper;
The LORD is your shade at your right hand.
The sun shall not strike you by day,
Nor the moon by night.

The LORD shall preserve you from all evil;
He shall preserve your soul.
The LORD shall preserve your going out and
your coming in
From this time forth, and even forevermore.

—PSALM 121

"I will go before you
And make the crooked places straight;
I will break in pieces the gates of bronze
And cut the bars of iron.

I will give you the treasures of darkness
    And hidden riches of secret places,
    That you may know that I, the LORD,
    Who call you by your name,
    Am the God of Israel.
For Jacob My servant's sake,
    And Israel My elect,
    I have even called you by your name;
    I have named you, though you have not
        known Me.
I am the LORD, and there is no other;
    There is no God besides Me.
    I will gird you, though you have not known Me,
That they may know from the rising of the
        sun to its setting
    That there is none besides Me.
    I am the LORD, and there is no other;
I form the light and create darkness,
    I make peace and create calamity;
    I, the LORD, do all these things."

—ISAIAH 45:2–7

The Power
of God Is . . .

Have you not known?
    Have you not heard?
    The everlasting God, the LORD,
    The Creator of the ends of the earth,
    Neither faints nor is weary.
    His understanding is unsearchable.
He gives power to the weak,
    And to those who have no might He
        increases strength.
Even the youths shall faint and be weary,
    And the young men shall utterly fall,
But those who wait on the LORD
    Shall renew their strength;
    They shall mount up with wings like eagles,
    They shall run and not be weary,
    They shall walk and not faint.

—ISAIAH 40:28–31

The Power of God Is
His Infallible Word

By faith we understand that the worlds were framed by the word of God, so that the things which are seen were not made of things which are visible.

—HEBREWS 11:3

In the beginning was the Word, and the Word was with God, and the Word was God. He was in the beginning with God.

All things were made through Him, and without Him nothing was made that was made. In Him was life, and the life was the light of men. And the light shines in the darkness, and the darkness did not comprehend it.

And the Word became flesh and dwelt among us, and we beheld His glory, the glory as of the only begotten of the Father, full of grace and truth.

—JOHN 1:1–5, 14

Forever, O LORD,
    Your word is settled in heaven.
Your faithfulness endures to all generations;
    You established the earth, and it abides.

Your word is a lamp to my feet
    And a light to my path.
I have sworn and confirmed
    That I will keep Your righteous judgments.

Your testimonies are wonderful;
    Therefore my soul keeps them.
The entrance of Your words gives light;
    It gives understanding to the simple.

—PSALM 119:89–90, 105–106, 129–130

I will praise You with my whole heart;
    Before the gods I will sing praises to You.
I will worship toward Your holy temple,
    And praise Your name
    For Your lovingkindness and Your truth;
    For You have magnified Your word above
        all Your name.

—PSALM 138:1–2

So then faith comes by hearing, and hearing
by the word of God.

—ROMANS 10:17

Your word is very pure;
Therefore Your servant loves it.

My eyes are awake through the night watches,
That I may meditate on Your word.

—PSALM 119:140, 148

For the word of the LORD is right,
And all His work is done in truth.
He loves righteousness and justice;
The earth is full of the goodness of the LORD.

By the word of the LORD the heavens were made,
And all the host of them by the breath of
His mouth.
He gathers the waters of the sea together as
a heap;
He lays up the deep in storehouses.

Let all the earth fear the LORD;
Let all the inhabitants of the world stand
in awe of Him.
For He spoke, and it was done;
He commanded, and it stood fast.

—PSALM 33:4–9

Therefore lay aside all filthiness and overflow of wickedness, and receive with meekness the implanted word, which is able to save your souls. But be doers of the word, and not hearers only, deceiving yourselves.

—JAMES 1:21–22

He who despises the word will be destroyed,
But he who fears the commandment will
be rewarded.
The law of the wise is a fountain of life,
To turn one away from the snares of death.
—PROVERBS 13:13–14

The Power of God Is
FAITH

Now faith is the substance of things hoped for, the evidence of things not seen.

By faith we understand that the worlds were framed by the word of God, so that the things which are seen were not made of things which are visible.

By faith Abel offered to God a more excellent sacrifice than Cain, through which he obtained witness that he was righteous, God testifying of his gifts; and through it he being dead still speaks.

By faith Enoch was taken away so that he did not see death, *"and was not found, because God had taken him"*; for before he was taken he had this testimony, that he pleased God. But without faith it is impossible to please Him, for he who comes to God must believe that He is, and that He is a rewarder of those who diligently seek Him.

By faith Noah, being divinely warned of things not yet seen, moved with godly fear, prepared an ark for the saving of his household, by which he condemned the world and became heir of the righteousness which is according to faith.

By faith Abraham obeyed when he was called to go out to the place which he would receive as an inheritance. And he went out, not knowing where he was going. By faith he dwelt in the land of promise as in a foreign country, dwelling in tents with Isaac and Jacob, the heirs with him of the same promise.

By faith Sarah herself also received strength to conceive seed, and she bore a child when she was past the age, because she judged Him faithful who had promised.

By faith Abraham, when he was tested, offered up Isaac, and he who had received the promises offered up his only begotten son.

—HEBREWS 11:1, 3–9, 11, 17

Therefore, having been justified by faith, we have peace with God through our Lord Jesus Christ, through whom also we have access by faith into this grace in which we stand, and rejoice in hope of the glory of God.

—ROMANS 5:1–2

But before faith came, we were kept under guard by the law, kept for the faith which would afterward be revealed. Therefore the law was our tutor to bring us to Christ, that we might be justified by faith. But after faith has come, we are no longer under a tutor.

For you are all sons of God through faith in Christ Jesus.

—Galatians 3:23–26

For by grace you have been saved through faith, and that not of yourselves; it is the gift of God, not of works, lest anyone should boast. For we are His workmanship, created in Christ Jesus for good works, which God prepared beforehand that we should walk in them.

—Ephesians 2:8–10

"For assuredly, I say to you, if you have faith as a mustard seed, you will say to this mountain, 'Move from here to there,' and it will move; and nothing will be impossible for you. However, this kind does not go out except by prayer and fasting."

—Matthew 17:20b–21

Now He who has prepared us for this very thing is God, who also has given us the Spirit as a guarantee.

So we are always confident, knowing that while we are at home in the body we are absent from the Lord. For we walk by faith, not by sight.

—2 CORINTHIANS 5:5—7

My brethren, count it all joy when you fall into various trials, knowing that the testing of your faith produces patience. But let patience have its perfect work, that you may be perfect and complete, lacking nothing.

—JAMES 1:2—4

So Jesus answered and said to them, "Have faith in God. For assuredly, I say to you, whoever says to this mountain, 'Be removed and be cast into the sea,' and does not doubt in his heart, but believes that those things he says will be done, he will have whatever he says. Therefore I say to you, whatever things you ask when you pray, believe that you receive them, and you will have them."

—MARK 11:22—24

The Power of God Is
SPIRITUAL AUTHORITY

For I am not ashamed of the gospel of
Christ, for it is the power of God to salvation
for everyone who believes, for the Jew first and
also for the Greek. For in it the righteousness
of God is revealed from faith to faith; as it is
written, *"The just shall live by faith."*

—ROMANS 1:16–17

He came to His own, and His own did not
receive Him. But as many as received Him, to
them He gave the right to become children of
God, to those who believe in His name: who
were born, not of blood, nor of the will of the
flesh, nor of the will of man, but of God.

And the Word became flesh and dwelt
among us, and we beheld His glory, the glory
as of the only begotten of the Father, full of
grace and truth.

—JOHN 1:11–14

Finally, my brethren, be strong in the Lord and in the power of His might. Put on the whole armor of God, that you may be able to stand against the wiles of the devil. For we do not wrestle against flesh and blood, but against principalities, against powers, against the rulers of the darkness of this age, against spiritual hosts of wickedness in the heavenly places. Therefore take up the whole armor of God, that you may be able to withstand in the evil day, and having done all, to stand. Stand therefore, having girded your waist with truth, having put on the breastplate of righteousness, and having shod your feet with the preparation of the gospel of peace; above all, taking the shield of faith with which you will be able to quench all the fiery darts of the wicked one. And take the helmet of salvation, and the sword of the Spirit, which is the word of God; praying always with all prayer and supplication in the Spirit, being watchful to this end with all perseverance and supplication for all the saints.

—EPHESIANS 6:10–18

Now then, we are ambassadors for Christ, as though God were pleading through us: we implore you on Christ's behalf, be reconciled to God. For He made Him who knew no sin to be sin for us, that we might become the righteousness of God in Him.

—2 CORINTHIANS 5:20–21

"Assuredly, I say to you, whatever you bind on earth will be bound in heaven, and whatever you loose on earth will be loosed in heaven.

Again I say to you that if two of you agree on earth concerning anything that they ask, it will be done for them by My Father in heaven. For where two or three are gathered together in My name, I am there in the midst of them."

—MATTHEW 18:18–20

For God has not given us a spirit of fear, but of power and of love and of a sound mind.

Therefore do not be ashamed of the testimony of our Lord, nor of me His prisoner, but share with me in the sufferings for the gospel according to the power of God.

—2 TIMOTHY 1:7–8

And what is the exceeding greatness of His power toward us who believe, according to the working of His mighty power which He worked in Christ when He raised Him from the dead and seated Him at His right hand in the heavenly places, far above all principality and power and might and dominion, and every name that is named, not only in this age but also in that which is to come. And He put all things under His feet, and gave Him to be head over all things to the church, which is His body, the fullness of Him who fills all in all.

—Ephesians 1:19–23

For though we walk in the flesh, we do not war according to the flesh. For the weapons of our warfare are not carnal but mighty in God for pulling down strongholds, casting down arguments and every high thing that exalts itself against the knowledge of God, bringing every thought into captivity to the obedience of Christ, and being ready to punish all disobedience when your obedience is fulfilled.

—2 Corinthians 10:3–6

The Power of God Is
HIS COVENANT

For we are His workmanship, created in Christ Jesus for good works, which God prepared beforehand that we should walk in them.

Therefore remember that you, once Gentiles in the flesh—who are called Uncircumcision by what is called the Circumcision made in the flesh by hands—that at that time you were without Christ, being aliens from the commonwealth of Israel and strangers from the covenants of promise, having no hope and without God in the world. But now in Christ Jesus you who once were far off have been brought near by the blood of Christ.

For He Himself is our peace, who has made both one, and has broken down the middle wall of separation, having abolished in His flesh the enmity, that is, the law of commandments contained in ordinances, so as to create in Himself one new man from the two, thus making peace.

—EPHESIANS 2:10–15

But now He has obtained a more excellent ministry, inasmuch as He is also Mediator of a better covenant, which was established on better promises.

For if that first covenant had been faultless, then no place would have been sought for a second. Because finding fault with them, He says: *"Behold, the days are coming, says the Lord, when I will make a new covenant with the house of Israel and with the house of Judah—not according to the covenant that I made with their fathers in the day when I took them by the hand to lead them out of the land of Egypt; because they did not continue in My covenant, and I disregarded them, says the Lord. For this is the covenant that I will make with the house of Israel after those days, says the Lord: I will put My laws in their mind and write them on their hearts; and I will be their God, and they shall be My people. None of them shall teach his neighbor, and none his brother, saying, 'Know the Lord,' for all shall know Me, from the least of them to the greatest of them. For I will be merciful to their unrighteousness, and their sins and their lawless deeds I will remember no more."* In that He says, *"A new covenant,"* He has made the first obsolete. Now what is becoming obsolete and growing old is ready to vanish away.

—HEBREWS 8:6–13

Brethren, I speak in the manner of men: Though it is only a man's covenant, yet if it is confirmed, no one annuls or adds to it. Now to Abraham and his Seed were the promises made. He does not say, "And to seeds," as of many, but as of one, *"And to your Seed,"* who is Christ. And this I say, that the law, which was four hundred and thirty years later, cannot annul the covenant that was confirmed before by God in Christ, that it should make the promise of no effect. For if the inheritance is of the law, it is no longer of promise; but God gave it to Abraham by promise.

What purpose then does the law serve? It was added because of transgressions, till the Seed should come to whom the promise was made; and it was appointed through angels by the hand of a mediator. Now a mediator does not mediate for one only, but God is one.

Is the law then against the promises of

God? Certainly not! For if there had been a law given which could have given life, truly righteousness would have been by the law. But the Scripture has confined all under sin, that the promise by faith in Jesus Christ might be given to those who believe.

But before faith came, we were kept under guard by the law, kept for the faith which would afterward be revealed. Therefore the law was our tutor to bring us to Christ, that we might be justified by faith. But after faith has come, we are no longer under a tutor.

For you are all sons of God through faith in Christ Jesus. For as many of you as were baptized into Christ have put on Christ. There is neither Jew nor Greek, there is neither slave nor free, there is neither male nor female; for you are all one in Christ Jesus. And if you are Christ's, then you are Abraham's seed, and heirs according to the promise.

—GALATIANS 3:15–29

For when God made a promise to Abraham, because He could swear by no one greater, He swore by Himself, saying, *"Surely blessing I will*

bless you, and multiplying I will multiply you."
And so, after he had patiently endured, he
obtained the promise.

For men indeed swear by the greater, and an
oath for confirmation is for them an end of all
dispute. Thus God, determining to show more
abundantly to the heirs of promise the
immutability of His counsel, confirmed it by
an oath, that by two immutable things, in
which it is impossible for God to lie, we might
have strong consolation, who have fled for
refuge to lay hold of the hope set before us.
This hope we have as an anchor of the soul,
both sure and steadfast, and which enters the
Presence behind the veil.

—HEBREWS 6:13–19

Who is the man that fears the LORD?
Him shall He teach in the way He chooses.
He himself shall dwell in prosperity,
And his descendants shall inherit the earth.
The secret of the LORD is with those who fear
Him,
And He will show them His covenant

—PSALM 25:12–14

How much more shall the blood of Christ, who through the eternal Spirit offered Himself without spot to God, cleanse your conscience from dead works to serve the living God?

And for this reason He is the Mediator of the new covenant, by means of death, for the redemption of the transgressions under the first covenant, that those who are called may receive the promise of the eternal inheritance.

—Hebrews 9:14–15

"Behold, the days are coming, says the Lord, when I will make a new covenant with the house of Israel and with the house of Judah— not according to the covenant that I made with their fathers in the day that I took them by the hand to lead them out of the land of Egypt, My covenant which they broke, though I was a husband to them, says the Lord. But this is the covenant that I will make with the house of Israel after those days, says the Lord: I will put My law in their minds, and write it on their hearts; and I will be their God, and they shall be My people."

—Jeremiah 31:31–33

The Power of God Is
HIS NEVER CHANGING PROMISE

For I know the thoughts that I think toward you, says the LORD, thoughts of peace and not of evil, to give you a future and a hope. Then you will call upon Me and go and pray to Me, and I will listen to you. And you will seek Me and find Me, when you search for Me with all your heart.

—JEREMIAH 29:11–13

"I am the vine, you are the branches. He who abides in Me, and I in him, bears much fruit; for without Me you can do nothing."

"If you abide in Me, and My words abide in you, you will ask what you desire, and it shall be done for you. By this My Father is glorified, that you bear much fruit; so you will be My disciples.

"As the Father loved Me, I also have loved you; abide in My love."

—JOHN 15:5, 7–9

Trust in the LORD with all your heart,
    And lean not on your own understanding;
In all your ways acknowledge Him,
    And He shall direct your paths.

—PROVERBS 3:5–6

Therefore, if anyone is in Christ, he is a new creation; old things have passed away; behold, all things have become new.

—2 CORINTHIANS 5:17

But this I say: He who sows sparingly will also reap sparingly, and he who sows bountifully will also reap bountifully. So let each one give as he purposes in his heart, not grudgingly or of necessity; for God loves a cheerful giver. And God is able to make all grace abound toward you, that you, always having all sufficiency in all things, may have an abundance for every good work.

—2 CORINTHIANS 9:6–8

And my God shall supply all your need according to His riches in glory by Christ Jesus.

—PHILIPPIANS 4:19

This is the message which we have heard from Him and declare to you, that God is light and in Him is no darkness at all. If we say that we have fellowship with Him, and walk in darkness, we lie and do not practice the truth. But if we walk in the light as He is in the light, we have fellowship with one another, and the blood of Jesus Christ His Son cleanses us from all sin.

—1 JOHN 1:5–7

Then Jesus said to those Jews who believed Him, "If you abide in My word, you are My disciples indeed. And you shall know the truth, and the truth shall make you free."

"Therefore if the Son makes you free, you shall be free indeed."

—JOHN 8:31–32, 36

The Love of God Is . . .

For the love of Christ compels us,
because we judge thus: that if One died
for all, then all died; and He died for all,
that those who live should live no longer
for themselves, but for Him who died for
them and rose again.

Therefore, if anyone is in Christ, he
is a new creation; old things have passed
away; behold, all things have become
new.

—2 CORINTHIANS 5:14–15, 17

The Love of God Is
YOUR ETERNAL INHERITANCE

But the Scripture has confined all under sin, that the promise by faith in Jesus Christ might be given to those who believe.

But before faith came, we were kept under guard by the law, kept for the faith which would afterward be revealed. Therefore the law was our tutor to bring us to Christ, that we might be justified by faith. But after faith has come, we are no longer under a tutor.

For you are all sons of God through faith in Christ Jesus. For as many of you as were baptized into Christ have put on Christ. There is neither Jew nor Greek, there is neither slave nor free, there is neither male nor female; for you are all one in Christ Jesus. And if you are Christ's, then you are Abraham's seed, and heirs according to the promise.

—GALATIANS 3:22–29

Blessed be the God and Father of our Lord Jesus Christ, who according to His abundant mercy has begotten us again to a living hope through the resurrection of Jesus Christ from the dead, to an inheritance incorruptible and undefiled and that does not fade away, reserved in heaven for you, who are kept by the power of God through faith for salvation ready to be revealed in the last time.

—1 PETER 1:3–5

In Him also we have obtained an inheritance, being predestined according to the purpose of Him who works all things according to the counsel of His will, that we who first trusted in Christ should be to the praise of His glory. In Him you also trusted, after you heard the word of truth, the gospel of your salvation; in whom also, having believed, you were sealed with the Holy Spirit of promise, who is the guarantee of our inheritance until the redemption of the purchased possession, to the praise of His glory.

—EPHESIANS 1:11–14

Now this I say, brethren, that flesh and blood cannot inherit the kingdom of God; nor does corruption inherit incorruption. Behold, I tell you a mystery: We shall not all sleep, but we shall all be changed—in a moment, in the twinkling of an eye, at the last trumpet. For the trumpet will sound, and the dead will be raised incorruptible, and we shall be changed. For this corruptible must put on incorruption, and this mortal must put on immortality. So when this corruptible has put on incorruption, and this mortal has put on immortality, then shall be brought to pass the saying that is written: *"Death is swallowed up in victory."*

"O Death, where is your sting?
O Hades, where is your victory?"

The sting of death is sin, and the strength of sin is the law. But thanks be to God, who gives us the victory through our Lord Jesus Christ.

Therefore, my beloved brethren, be steadfast, immovable, always abounding in the work of the Lord, knowing that your labor is not in vain in the Lord.

—1 Corinthians 15:50–58

Then He who sat on the throne said, "Behold, I make all things new." And He said to me, "Write, for these words are true and faithful."

And He said to me, "It is done! I am the Alpha and the Omega, the Beginning and the End. I will give of the fountain of the water of life freely to him who thirsts. He who overcomes shall inherit all things, and I will be his God and he shall be My son."

—REVELATION 21:5–7

He has delivered us from the power of darkness and conveyed us into the kingdom of the Son of His love, in whom we have redemption through His blood, the forgiveness of sins.

He is the image of the invisible God, the firstborn over all creation. For by Him all things were created that are in heaven and that are on earth, visible and invisible, whether thrones or dominions or principalities or powers. All things were created through Him and for Him.

—COLOSSIANS 1:13–16

Now I say that the heir, as long as he is a child, does not differ at all from a slave, though he is master of all, but is under guardians and stewards until the time appointed by the father. Even so we, when we were children, were in bondage under the elements of the world. But when the fullness of the time had come, God sent forth His Son, born of a woman, born under the law, to redeem those who were under the law, that we might receive the adoption as sons. And because you are sons, God has sent forth the Spirit of His Son into your hearts, crying out, "Abba, Father!" Therefore you are no longer a slave but a son, and if a son, then an heir of God through Christ.

—GALATIANS 4:1–7

The Love of God Is
HEALING FOR YOUR LIFE

The LORD builds up Jerusalem;
    He gathers together the outcasts of Israel.
He heals the brokenhearted
    And binds up their wounds.
He counts the number of the stars;
    He calls them all by name.
Great is our Lord, and mighty in power;
    His understanding is infinite.
The LORD lifts up the humble;
    He casts the wicked down to the ground.

—PSALM 147:2–6

Have mercy on me, O LORD, for I am weak;
    O LORD, heal me, for my bones are troubled.
My soul also is greatly troubled;
    But You, O LORD—how long?

Return, O LORD, deliver me!
    Oh, save me for Your mercies' sake!
For in death there is no remembrance of You;
    In the grave who will give You thanks?

—PSALM 6:2–5

"The Spirit of the Lord GOD is upon Me,
  Because the LORD has anointed Me
  To preach good tidings to the poor;
  He has sent Me to heal the brokenhearted,
  To proclaim liberty to the captives,
  And the opening of the prison to those
      who are bound;
To proclaim the acceptable year of the LORD,
  And the day of vengeance of our God;
  To comfort all who mourn,
To console those who mourn in Zion,
  To give them beauty for ashes,
  The oil of joy for mourning,
  The garment of praise for the spirit of
      heaviness;
  That they may be called trees of righteousness,
  The planting of the LORD, that He may be
      glorified."

—ISAIAH 61:1–3

"I, even I, am He who comforts you.
  Who are you that you should be afraid
  Of a man who will die,
  And of the son of a man who will be made
      like grass?"

—ISAIAH 51:12

Is anyone among you sick? Let him call for the elders of the church, and let them pray over him, anointing him with oil in the name of the Lord. And the prayer of faith will save the sick, and the Lord will raise him up. And if he has committed sins, he will be forgiven. Confess your trespasses to one another, and pray for one another, that you may be healed. The effective, fervent prayer of a righteous man avails much.

—JAMES 5:14–16

Surely He has borne our griefs
    And carried our sorrows;
    Yet we esteemed Him stricken,
    Smitten by God, and afflicted.
But He was wounded for our transgressions,
    He was bruised for our iniquities;
    The chastisement for our peace was upon
        Him,
    And by His stripes we are healed.
All we like sheep have gone astray;
    We have turned, every one, to his own way;
    And the LORD has laid on Him the iniquity
        of us all.

—ISAIAH 53:4–6

"The Spirit of the LORD is upon Me,
*   Because He has anointed Me*
*   To preach the gospel to the poor;*
*   He has sent Me to heal the brokenhearted,*
*   To proclaim liberty to the captives*
*   And recovery of sight to the blind,*
To set at liberty those who are oppressed;
*   To proclaim the acceptable year of the LORD."*

—LUKE 4:18–19

Bless the LORD, O my soul;
    And all that is within me, bless His holy
        name!
Bless the LORD, O my soul,
    And forget not all His benefits:
Who forgives all your iniquities,
    Who heals all your diseases,
Who redeems your life from destruction,
    Who crowns you with lovingkindness and
        tender mercies,
Who satisfies your mouth with good things,
    So that your youth is renewed like the eagle's.

—PSALM 103:1–5

Blessed be the God and Father of our Lord Jesus Christ, the Father of mercies and God of all comfort, who comforts us in all our tribulation, that we may be able to comfort those who are in any trouble, with the comfort with which we ourselves are comforted by God. For as the sufferings of Christ abound in us, so our consolation also abounds through Christ.

—2 CORINTHIANS 1:3–5

The Love of God Is
THE GOODNESS OF GOD

Oh, how great is Your goodness,
    Which You have laid up for those who
        fear You,
    Which You have prepared for those who
        trust in You
    In the presence of the sons of men!
You shall hide them in the secret place of
        Your presence
    From the plots of man;
    You shall keep them secretly in a pavilion
    From the strife of tongues.

—PSALM 31:19–20

Oh, that men would give thanks to the LORD
        for His goodness,
    And for His wonderful works to the children
        of men!
For He satisfies the longing soul,
    And fills the hungry soul with goodness.

—PSALM 107:8–9

For the word of the LORD is right,
    And all His work is done in truth.
He loves righteousness and justice;
    The earth is full of the goodness of the LORD.

By the word of the LORD the heavens were made,
    And all the host of them by the breath
        of His mouth.
He gathers the waters of the sea together as
        a heap;
    He lays up the deep in storehouses.

Let all the earth fear the LORD;
    Let all the inhabitants of the world stand
        in awe of Him.
For He spoke, and it was done;
    He commanded, and it stood fast.

—PSALM 33:4–9

For the LORD God is a sun and shield;
    The LORD will give grace and glory;
    No good thing will He withhold
    From those who walk uprightly.

O LORD of hosts,
    Blessed is the man who trusts in You!

—PSALM 84:11–12

How precious is Your lovingkindness, O God!
    Therefore the children of men put their
        trust under the shadow of Your wings.
They are abundantly satisfied with the fullness
        of Your house,
    And You give them drink from the river of
        Your pleasures.
For with You is the fountain of life;
    In Your light we see light.

—Psalm 36:7–9

The Lord has been mindful of us;
    He will bless us;
    He will bless the house of Israel;
    He will bless the house of Aaron.
He will bless those who fear the Lord,
    Both small and great.

May the Lord give you increase more and more,
    You and your children.
May you be blessed by the Lord,
    Who made heaven and earth.

—Psalm 115:12–15

The works of the LORD are great,
    Studied by all who have pleasure in them.
His work is honorable and glorious,
    And His righteousness endures forever.
He has made His wonderful works to be
        remembered;
    The LORD is gracious and full of compassion.
—PSALM 111:2–4

For I am persuaded that neither death nor
life, nor angels nor principalities nor powers,
nor things present nor things to come, nor
height nor depth, nor any other created thing,
shall be able to separate us from the love of
God which is in Christ Jesus our Lord.
—ROMANS 8:38–39

The Love of God Is
For Your Unsaved Loved Ones

That if you confess with your mouth the Lord Jesus and believe in your heart that God has raised Him from the dead, you will be saved. For with the heart one believes unto righteousness, and with the mouth confession is made unto salvation. For the Scripture says, *"Whoever believes on Him will not be put to shame."*

—Romans 10:9–11

But God, who is rich in mercy, because of His great love with which He loved us, even when we were dead in trespasses, made us alive together with Christ (by grace you have been saved), and raised us up together, and made us sit together in the heavenly places in Christ Jesus, that in the ages to come He might show the exceeding riches of His grace in His kindness toward us in Christ Jesus. For by grace you have been saved through faith, and that not of yourselves; it is the gift of God, not of works, lest anyone should boast.

—Ephesians 2:4–9

There is therefore now no condemnation to those who are in Christ Jesus, who do not walk according to the flesh, but according to the Spirit. For the law of the Spirit of life in Christ Jesus has made me free from the law of sin and death. For what the law could not do in that it was weak through the flesh, God did by sending His own Son in the likeness of sinful flesh, on account of sin: He condemned sin in the flesh, that the righteous requirement of the law might be fulfilled in us who do not walk according to the flesh but according to the Spirit.

For those who live according to the flesh set their minds on the things of the flesh, but those who live according to the Spirit, the things of the Spirit.

—Romans 8:1–5

Blessed be the Lord,
    Who daily loads us with benefits,
    The God of our salvation!
Our God is the God of salvation;
    And to God the Lord belong escapes from
        death.

—Psalm 68:19–20

For none of us lives to himself, and no one dies to himself. For if we live, we live to the Lord; and if we die, we die to the Lord. Therefore, whether we live or die, we are the Lord's.

For to this end Christ died and rose and lived again, that He might be Lord of both the dead and the living. But why do you judge your brother? Or why do you show contempt for your brother? For we shall all stand before the judgment seat of Christ. For it is written:

*"As I live, says the L*ORD*,*
Every knee shall bow to Me,
And every tongue shall confess to God."

So then each of us shall give account of himself to God.

Therefore let us not judge one another anymore, but rather resolve this, not to put a stumbling block or a cause to fall in our brother's way.

—ROMANS 14:7–13

The steps of a good man are ordered by the LORD,
    And He delights in his way.
Though he fall, he shall not be utterly cast down;
    For the LORD upholds him with His hand.

—PSALM 37:23–24

And Jesus said to them, "I am the bread of life. He who comes to Me shall never hunger, and he who believes in Me shall never thirst. But I said to you that you have seen Me and yet do not believe. All that the Father gives Me will come to Me, and the one who comes to Me I will by no means cast out. For I have come down from heaven, not to do My own will, but the will of Him who sent Me. This is the will of the Father who sent Me, that of all He has given Me I should lose nothing, but should raise it up at the last day. And this is the will of Him who sent Me, that everyone who sees the Son and believes in Him may have everlasting life; and I will raise him up at the last day."

—JOHN 6:35–40

"Assuredly, I say to you, unless you are converted and become as little children, you will by no means enter the kingdom of heaven. Therefore whoever humbles himself as this little child is the greatest in the kingdom of heaven.

"Whoever receives one little child like this in My name receives Me. But whoever causes one of these little ones who believe in Me to sin, it would be better for him if a millstone were hung around his neck, and he were drowned in the depth of the sea.

"Woe to the world because of offenses! For offenses must come, but woe to that man by whom the offense comes! If your hand or foot causes you to sin, cut it off and cast it from you. It is better for you to enter into life lame or maimed, rather than having two hands or two feet, to be cast into the everlasting fire. And if your eye causes you to sin, pluck it out and cast it from you. It is better for you to enter into life with one eye, rather than having two eyes, to be cast into hell fire.

"Take heed that you do not despise one of these little ones, for I say to you that in heaven their angels always see the face of My Father who is in heaven. For the Son of Man has come to save that which was lost.

"What do you think? If a man has a hundred sheep, and one of them goes astray, does he not leave the ninety-nine and go to the mountains to seek the one that is straying? And if he should find it, assuredly, I say to you, he rejoices more over that sheep than over the ninety-nine that did not go astray. Even so it is not the will of your Father who is in heaven that one of these little ones should perish.

"Moreover if your brother sins against you, go and tell him his fault between you and him alone. If he hears you, you have gained your brother."

—MATTHEW 18:3–15

Prayer List

Prayer List

Prayer List

Prayer List